Ashley Tisdale

Life Is Sweet!

An Unauthorized Biography
by Grace Norwich

PRICE STERN SLOAN
Published by the Penguin Group
Penguin Group (USA) Inc., 375 Hudson Street,
New York, New York 10014, U.S.A.
Penguin Group (Canada), 90 Eglinton Avenue East, Suite 700,
Toronto, Ontario, Canada M4P 2Y3
(a division of Pearson Penguin Canada Inc.)
Penguin Books Ltd, 80 Strand, London WC2R 0RL, England
Penguin Ireland, 25 St Stephens Green, Dublin 2, Ireland
(a division of Penguin Books Ltd)
Penguin Group (Australia), 250 Camberwell Road,
Camberwell, Victoria 3124, Australia
(a division of Pearson Australia Group Pty Ltd)
Penguin Books India Pvt Ltd, 11 Community Centre,
Panchsheel Park, New Delhi - 110 017, India
Penguin Group (NZ), Cnr Airborne and Rosedale Roads,
Albany, Auckland 1310, New Zealand
(a division of Pearson New Zealand Ltd)
Penguin Books (South Africa) (Pty) Ltd, 24 Sturdee Avenue,
Rosebank, Johannesburg 2196, South Africa

Penguin Books Ltd, Registered Offices:
80 Strand, London WC2R 0RL, England

Photo credits: Cover: courtesy of Jeffery Mayer/Star File. Insert photos: first page,
third page, and fourth page courtesy of Jeffery Mayer/Star File; second page
courtesy of Walt Disney Television/Photofest © Walt Disney Television. Cover
and insert background courtesy of mayang.com.

Library of Congress Control Number: 2006020967

ISBN 0-8431-2183-1   10 9 8 7 6 5 4

Ashley Tisdale
Life Is Sweet!

An Unauthorized Biography
by Grace Norwich

PSS!
PRICE STERN SLOAN

Contents

Introduction: The Sweet Life of Ashley Tisdale   5

1   Fun Fast Facts   6

2   Down-to-Earth Star   10

3   Jersey Girl   16

4   Catching a Star . . . in the Mall   22

5   Résumé Building   31

6   Too Suite for Words   40

7   Home Away from Home: Life on *The Suite Life*   47

8   *High School Musical*, Here We Come!   57

9   Drama Queen   62

10   Straight to the Head of the Class   73

11   Keeping It Real   85

12   Future Tense   93

13   Ashley's Style File   101

14   Lucky Stars   111

15   By the Numbers   117

16   Are You an Ashley Expert?   123

17   Internet Resources   126

18   The End of the Beginning   128

Introduction
The Sweet Life of Ashley Tisdale

Ashley Tisdale is far from just another pretty Hollywood face! A solid triple threat with an amazing vocal range, dance skills, and great acting chops, Ashley is a superstar in the making. But this beautiful and talented star of the hit Disney Channel show *The Suite Life of Zack & Cody* and the phenomenally successful Disney Channel movie *High School Musical* has her head on straight. While other stars her age are out club-hopping and gunning for spots in *Us Weekly* and *OK!*, Ashley can be found hanging out in her condo with her mom and her puppy. But don't let her laid-back demeanor fool you. Ashley is one powerhouse of a performer who can morph from character to character without batting an eyelash. It's been a long road, but even though she's living the sweet life now, Ashley is still the girl-next-door from New Jersey that she was when she started out.

Chapter 1
Fun Fast Facts

You're Ashley's number-one fan. You never miss an episode of *The Suite Life* and you've seen *High School Musical* a thousand times. You don't even need the DVD sing-along version to belt out the musical numbers. And now you're reading this book. So you think you know everything there is to know about Ashley? Well, check out these essential biographical details to make sure that you have your Ashley Tisdale facts straight.

1. Name: Ashley Michelle Tisdale

2. Birthday: July 2, 1985

3. Birthplace: West Deal, New Jersey

4. Height: 5 feet 3 inches

5. Eyes: Brown

6. Current home: Valencia, California

7. Zodiac sign: Cancer

8. Parents: Lisa and Mike Tisdale

9. Siblings: Older sis, Jennifer Tisdale (also an actress and her closest friend)

10. Famous relatives: Grandfather Arnold Morris, who made Ginsu knives popular, and cousin Ron Popeil, an inventor

11. Favorite color: Pink

12. Favorite food: Sushi, but absolutely no eel—ever!

13. Food she can't live without: Peanut Butter Cap'n Crunch and vanilla ice blend from Coffee Bean. Ashley can't start her morning without either.

14. Her hidden talent: She loves to go horseback riding!

15. The name of Ashley's pet Maltipoo puppy: Blondie—it actually comes from Ashley's own nickname on *The Suite Life*.

16. Favorite books: *The Great Gatsby,* by F. Scott Fitzgerald. Ashley loves to read and sneaks little moments on set to dig into a good book. Sometimes she indulges in more fun fiction, like the series *The A-List,* by Zoey Dean. "It's kind of like *Laguna Beach* set in a book in Beverly Hills," she told teenhollywood.com. That's right up Ashley's alley.

17. Favorite music: Ashley loves Billy Joel as a solo artist, but her new favorite band is The Used.

18. Favorite car: A silver Range Rover

19. Favorite movie: *Peter Pan,* with Jeremy Sumpter. She's crazy for Tinkerbell (when she isn't watching chick flicks about weddings, or *Laguna Beach* on TV).

20. Favorite actors: Brittany Murphy, Julia Roberts, Johnny Depp, and Leonardo DiCaprio

21. Why Ashley loves acting: She can shed her image and become whomever she wants to be, as she told her official website, ashleytisdale.com: "I get to be different characters that tell different stories."

Chapter 2

Down-to-Earth Star

Ashley Tisdale has become a world-class celebrity by playing the girl you love to hate, Sharpay Evans, in the mega-hit Disney movie *High School Musical*. But in reality, the young actress is one of the sweetest stars you could ever know.

Sure, she's beautiful and blond, with a closet full of amazing clothes (well, maybe more like three or four closets). She is so famous that people ask for her autograph wherever she goes, and sometimes groups of kids chant her name when she hits hot rock concerts. She has producers and directors knocking down her door to read their scripts, and she makes plenty of money.

But Ashley doesn't let any of that go to her head. Despite all the glitz and glamour of her everyday existence, which has been made increasingly complicated with her rising stardom, she relishes the simple things in life, like hanging out with friends, doing creative things, shopping, and just flashing that big smile of hers when she launches into one of her favorite activities: laughing.

"I'm really nice and sweet. If you see me, you can totally come up to me. I'll totally say hi," Ashley said in 2005 to thestarscoop.com. "I'm really funny. I try to make people laugh. I love to make people laugh. It's, like, such a cool thing in the world to have people smile and laugh at me."

Yeah, that's right. Ashley will do pretty much anything for a laugh, and she isn't too famous to laugh at herself.

Ashley gets her humility from the fact that she hasn't always been a star. She understands what it means to be quiet, far from the center of attention. Even though now she's a successful actress, Ashley was actually really timid and reserved when she was a young kid. She was anything but the class clown while growing up in suburban New Jersey.

But there was a spark in Ashley, that something special, as they say in the business. Her acting talents and great face for the small screen were discovered soon enough. Ashley launched a career and moved to California with her family to be closer to the action. Although now she has relocated to the land of convertibles and skim double lattes, appeared on television and on magazine covers, and gained millions of adoring fans, Ashley has never forgotten her roots. She has even worked at a store at the mall, just like any normal teen!

Because she's super-close with her family, her parents and big sister, Jennifer, are always on hand to put her in her place if she ever gets too high on herself. Not that she needs it, since she's so down to earth. They are there for good stuff as well, like offering a shoulder (or shoulders) to cry on if she doesn't get a part. As the baby of the family, Ashley still relies on her family a lot. When she flies, she gets so nervous that she has to have her mom and her stuffed animal with her.

A celebrity who travels with her mom and a stuffed animal? Ashley definitely gives off a wholesome image, and she's not ashamed of that. In fact, that's exactly what she wants to portray. She's a different kind of star from the typical young actress or musician who gives off a bad-girl image, wearing seductive outfits, writhing around on videos, and freaking out at public events. Ashley rebels against this mode of celebrity. She loves clothes just as much as the next celebrity, but you'll never see her in boy shorts, belly-baring shirts, and stilettos. No stomach or tongue piercing for this ingénue. Ashley dresses modestly. Her style is tasteful but supercool. Her long, glossy blond hair, designer duds, and winning smile even attracted the sophisticated *New York Times* Style section, which singled her out for a fantastic wardrobe that suits her age. Modesty certainly works for Ashley. Lots of girls aspire to be like her, and luckily she's someone worthy of role-model status.

When Ashley auditioned for the Disney Channel's *The Suite Life of Zack & Cody,* a sitcom about twin boys who live in a hotel, she actually tried out for the part of the spoiled and snobby hotel owner's daughter, London Tipton. She also auditioned to play the role of the lovable babysitter and candy-counter clerk, Maddie Fitzpatrick, which of course eventually became the part that would make her famous. It's not just pure fate or luck that Ashley hit it big playing the character of Maddie, who is as sweet as the treats she sells. No, Ashley was totally psyched that she landed the part of a positive, happy character over a mean teen because it fit with her true personality. Maddie's sunny disposition was something she could totally relate to, and you know what they say about acting, writing, or art: Start with what you know.

That gave Ashley a great base to work from and allowed her to go on to roles that would challenge her range of acting, like that of Sharpay. But even though in *High School*

Musical she plays someone with a lot of attitude, it's still a Disney production, just like *The Suite Life of Zack & Cody*. And Disney is a company Ashley definitely feels really secure and content working for. Just take a look at the example of *High School Musical* alone. While the musical phenomenon has been compared to huge hits of the past, such as *Grease* or *Dirty Dancing*, the Disney movie differs in that it doesn't have any sex, drugs, bad language, and, oh yeah, cigarettes.

A lot of people think that *High School Musical*'s old-fashioned take on teens is the reason it has become a pop culture sensation. Even though celebrities like Britney Spears, Christina Aguilera, and Jessica Simpson made names for themselves by acting sexy at an early age, a lot of kids just want to be, well, kids. "There's only one kiss in the film, and it's on the cheek. Its success contradicts the perception people have of kids being jaded, oversexualized, and more sophisticated than their age," explained children's marketing expert Chris Byrne to the *Chicago Sun-Times* in 2006. "It speaks to the inherent innocence of children."

Let's face it, you can't get much more innocent than the company that gave birth to Mickey Mouse. Ashley says that Disney is a perfect match for her age and her artistic sensibility.

"I love Disney because I'm really, really young still. I never really felt comfortable, even before I was on Disney, doing any type of roles that are really mature," she said in an interview to thestarscoop.com. "I always want to work for Disney my whole life. It keeps you with such a safe feeling that, you know, you don't have to show skin or do any of that stuff. It's comfortable, and I love the characters I portray. I figure this is where I want to be right now. I don't want to do all those mature roles right now. I have my whole life to do that."

So Ashley is an old-fashioned star, or maybe a new breed of star. The point is, she's a great girl. She's best buds with her folks, looks out for her costars, appreciates her fans, and understands that she needs to give it her all if she wants to stay on top in her demanding career. But maybe the best thing about Ashley is that she believes in dreams, not just for herself but for everyone else, too. Just like the message offered in *High School Musical*, Ashley believes fantasies can come true. "Always follow your dreams!" she told KriSeLen.com. "But remember you have to work hard. You can't expect it to be given to you. But never give up because you can do anything you want."

Chapter 3

Jersey Girl

Ashley Tisdale was born on July 2, 1985, in Monmouth County, New Jersey. Her parents, Lisa and Mike, glowed with pride when they brought their beautiful, brown-eyed girl home from the hospital to the family house in the town of West Deal. This is a typical all-American community, with lots of tree-lined streets, pretty parks, and freshwater lakes, with the Atlantic Ocean not too far away. It's also just a couple of hours' drive from New York City and the bright lights of Broadway, where Ashley would one day see her name lit up. But all that would have to wait.

Ashley's younger years were about as normal as they come. Her parents were definitely the doting types, showering lots of love and affection on Ashley and her older sister, Jennifer, who would also go on to be an actress. Obviously the two girls were used to getting a lot of attention from an early age, or they wouldn't be so comfortable performing onstage and in front of the camera as young women.

Actually, fame and celebrity are sort of in Ashley's blood. Her grandfather on her mother's side, Arnold Morris, is famous for developing Ginsu knives. In case you aren't a big cook, these are the supersharp knives that used to be advertised all the time on late-night "infomercials." These hammy commercials featured chefs in big hats using the knives to do all sorts of unbelievable things, like cutting tin cans in half and slicing rubber auto parts. (Okay, so none of that's as cool as starring in a Broadway musical and in a hit show on the Disney Channel, but still, Grandpa was pretty well-known in his time—just ask your own grandparents!)

Ashley is also related to another "famous" inventor named Ronald Popeil, though his inventions are even wackier than the Ginsu knives that cut through anything. For instance, maybe you've heard of a nifty little contraption called the Veg-O-Matic food slicer? Or the Popeil Pocket Fisherman? Or the Inside-the-Shell Egg Scrambler? No? Well, believe it or not, they're all the brainchildren of one of Ashley's distant relatives.

Growing up in New Jersey, Ashley did a lot of the same things kids in towns across America do. That included spending tons of time with her parents and her older and equally cute sister Jennifer. In fact, on the official Ashley Tisdale website, ashleytisdale.com, the star doesn't have to think for a second about what her one true favorite thing in the world is: "My family!" she declared. In another interview, this time with the *Miami Herald,* in 2005, Ashley was asked who was the most influential person in her life. She replied, "My mom. She has helped me get where I am today. She is my support and my best friend. I love her."

While the Tisdale parents must have sensed that Ashley (and her sister, too) had plenty of star potential, they were careful about instilling really positive values in their children. Growing up, the Tisdale girls definitely had none of the pampering that the characters Zack and Cody are used to on *The Suite Life*. Just the opposite. "I always had a normal life," Ashley explained to *American Cheerleader* in February 2006. "I worked at Wet Seal in the mall and went to a regular school. My dad wanted me to know how long it took to make money and not to take anything for granted." (If you're wondering, Wet Seal is a store that sells women's casual sportswear, which might explain where Ashley got her rockin' fashion sense.)

School was always a priority in the Tisdale household. Though Ashley no doubt spent a lot of hours hanging out with friends and shopping at the nearby mall (when she didn't have to work there, that is), the fun activities would have only been allowed after her homework was done. "My dad is adamant about education," Ashley told celeb101.com. "My sister graduated from college, and I cut a deal with him. He agreed to let me film some pilots as long as I took as many classes in music and acting as I could."

It was obvious from an early age that Ashley was blessed with loads of musical talent. Besides having an amazing voice, she also proved to be pretty good with instruments. "I have a really good ear with music," she said during an interview with *Scholastic News* online. "I can play piano by ear, which means I can listen to a song and play it on the piano. Melodies just kind of come up in my head. I have a voice teacher who showed me how [to write] lyrics." (Listen up, any of you aspiring performers who dread going to piano lessons each week. Lessons definitely helped turn Ashley into the mega-huge star she is today!)

Despite these natural musical abilities and her gift for

acting that Ashley is so well-known for today, she was actually more studious than you might expect. You can just as easily picture her with her nose buried in a book in school as you can imagine her belting out show tunes on stage. "My favorite subject was English or creative writing," she confirmed on ashleytisdale.com. "We did poems and made a magazine and I did one on celebrities. I called it *Celebrity Life* magazine." Obviously she had plenty of smarts *and* a desire to be famous.

Ashley was also a lot more reserved than most of the characters she went on to play on television. "When I was in school I was friendly with everybody," she told *Scholastic News* online, describing the difference between herself and Sharpay, the often mean-spirited character she played in *High School Musical*. "Believe it or not I was kind of quiet—I get that from my dad. My mom is really outgoing."

In addition to being a little on the shy side, it sounds like Ashley could be a bit of a klutz, as well. Talking to teenhollywood.com about one of her embarrassing moments, Ashley shares this story: "I was in school and I was running in P.E.—two miles! We were running on the sidewalk and I saw some cute guy on the other side of the street and I ran into a fire hydrant and flipped over it and landed on the sidewalk and the sprinklers were on, so I got soaked." Talk about doing flips for a boy!

So what happened? How did Ashley turn from this shy kid who used to run into things to a suave, sophisticated superstar with millions of adoring fans? Well, the loving parents and supportive home life were definitely a huge part of it. But she also credits one of America's oldest pastimes with making her more outgoing: cheerleading. "My sister was a hard-core cheerleader, and I always wanted to follow her," Ashley said in an interview with *American Cheerleader*. "I was really shy when I was younger, and cheerleading helped me come out of my shell."

Ashley was about eight years old the first time she put on her own cheerleader uniform. Something about getting up in front of hundreds of fans and rallying their support with nothing more than a smile and a pair of pom-poms unleashed the spirit of performance in her. But as we'll see in the next chapter, the performer in Ashley had already been there for some time. She just needed a good, loud cheer to bring it to life.

Chapter 4

Catching a Star ... in the Mall

It's pretty easy to imagine the scene that day at the Monmouth Mall in Eatontown, New Jersey, back in 1988. The place was no doubt bustling with shoppers, many of them local teenagers wearing neon stockings and the black rubber bracelets that were all the rage in the '80s. But the atmosphere was probably even a little crazier than normal on this particular afternoon, because Bill Perlman, owner of New Talent Management, was conducting a talent search—and he'd chosen the Monmouth Mall as the venue.

Just picture all the young guys and gals lined up, waiting for their audition with the judges. Remember, this was before the days of *American Idol* (or even the Internet), so the feeling must have been that this was their one big shot at stardom.

One person who did not seem very fazed by all the excitement was Ashley Tisdale. But then, she was just a three-year-old being pushed in a stroller through the corridors of the mall by her mother, Lisa. Still, even if Ashley and her mom may not have noticed the event Perlman was putting on, Perlman definitely noticed them. "She had a head full of beautiful curly hair, huge eyes, and when she looked at me, she made the hugest of smiles," Perlman recalled in an interview for the *Asbury Park Press* in 2006. "I followed her into the store and asked if they were going to be participating in the talent show. I was told, 'Not interested, but thanks.' I left them to their shopping knowing with certainty that she had no idea what I could do for them or what she was missing."

Successful talent agents don't get very far in this world by letting a sure thing get away, and Perlman was no different. So when he saw Ashley and her mom later that same day in the mall, he slipped her mom a business card, just on the off chance that she should happen to change her mind. A month or so later, Ashley's mom got in touch with Perlman. Not long after that, Ashley was going on her first audition. True to Perlman's predictions, she nailed it, and landed her first job modeling clothes for JCPenney. Even at three years old, Ashley was already ahead of the trends—it's no wonder she's so stylin' now! Though according to Perlman, Ashley's success goes beyond a big smile and flair for fashion. As he told the *Asbury*

Park Press, "The rest [of Ashley's success] has been lots of good fortune and plenty of work, preparation, and planning."

On the strength of her solid performance in the JCPenney spot, Ashley's commercial career took off and she went on to appear in over one hundred ads nationwide. There are too many to recall, but one in particular stands out from the rest, as much for Ashley's costar as for the product they were selling. That's the T-Mobile television commercial she made with Catherine Zeta-Jones, the gorgeous A-list actress who has been in such films as *The Mask of Zorro*, *Oceans Twelve,* and *Chicago*. She's also married to the equally famous actor, Michael Douglas. Ashley was pretty impressed by Zeta-Jones. When KriSeLen.com asked Ashley about her fondest memory from her commercial, she said, "It was the best experience. For four days I went to Canada and got to work with Catherine Zeta-Jones! She's so nice. It was so much fun!" Apparently, Zeta-Jones took quite a shine to her young bubbly counterpart as well. "At the time, I had curly hair and she'd compliment me on it," Ashley told *People* magazine.

That comment might surprise Ashley's fans, who are used to the pin-straight golden tresses she wears for most of her acting roles and in so many of the photo shoots she does.

But as her personal and professional stylist, Ozlem Dalgic, told *Sophisticate's Hairstyle*: "Ashley naturally has very thick, coarse, curly hair." So you see, just because you were born with one head of hair doesn't mean you can't play around with different dos.

Despite all the success Ashley was having with her acting career, she was the same regular girl at home in New Jersey. Her routine still consisted of the same things: schoolwork, piano lessons, and cheerleading during the week; hanging out with friends and maybe doing a little bit of shopping on the weekends. Her peers and teachers definitely weren't treating her like she was special.

In fact, though Tisdale was now working pretty steadily as a professional actor, she still wasn't landing many plum roles at school. "I didn't get along too well with the drama teachers," Ashley told the *Asbury Park Press* in 2006. "They never wanted to cast me in any parts." But even Ashley admits that the situation was a little tense with her teachers, given that she was often busy (and away from school) attending big city auditions. "I think they didn't like me going on the auditions, so I never got selected for the plays."

If Ashley was bothered about being passed over by the

drama teachers at school, she definitely forgot all about it when, at the age of eight, she was awarded the dream role of Cosette in *Les Misérables* on Broadway. This musical, by Alain Boublil and Claude-Michel Schönberg, with lyrics by Herbert Kretzmer, is one of the most popular and long-running musicals of all time. Opening in London in 1985, *Les Mis*, as it's known, tells the story of a man who is sent to prison for stealing a loaf of bread so that he can feed his family. When the play made it to Broadway two years later, it won eight Tony Awards, including Best Musical. Cosette is a featured part, that of the man's adopted young daughter.

Everything came together smoothly for Ashley when she went out for the role of Cosette. Although singing professionally posed a big challenge, it would launch an entire new side of her career. "Lacey Chabert had been starring in it, and she is one of my really good friends," Ashley told *Scholastic News* online. "She is older than I am and I looked up to her, and I thought she was really cool. I told my manager and he got me an audition for the national tour. My mom threw me into some voice lessons to get me prepared for it. It was a really great experience, and so I have sung ever since then. I love to sing."

Ashley enjoyed playing the part of Cosette so much that she stuck with it from 1993 to 1995. "It was amazing," she told KriSeLen.com. "I think it helped me get to the place where I am today." Not only did she have to memorize lines and learn to sing for a Broadway audience, she also had to perform every day (sometimes even twice a day if there was a matinee) for two years. It took so much energy to perform so often that she didn't have the strength to get nervous. Well, at least after a while. About being in *Les Misérables*, she said, "It taught me discipline and helped me get over being shy. I love doing comedy because it reminds me of theater; you get to perform in front of a live audience."

Performing in front of a live audience would prove to be an invaluable experience to Ashley down the line when she would go on to do television, where actors not only tape in front of a live audience, they also have to work day in and day out like professionals do on Broadway. And getting over her stage jitters only helped Ashley with her confidence when she went to auditions for commercials and TV appearances. Right after her stint in *Les Misérables*, Ashley landed another seminal American play: *Annie*. The original musical—based on an old-fashioned popular comic strip by Harold Gray, called *Little Orphan Annie*—first opened on Broadway at the Alvin Theatre on April 21, 1977, and ran for 2,377 performances! With music by Charles Strouse, lyrics by Martin Charnin, and dialogue by Thomas Meehan, the show, about ten-year-old Annie, who lives in an orphanage in Depression-era New York City, was a massive hit. Audiences fell in love with the little girl with the head of red curls. Every girl wanted to sing and act just like Andrea McArdle, the actress who played the original Annie. The success of the show was reflected in all the professional acclaim it received. *Annie* was nominated for eleven Tony Awards and won seven, including Best Musical. It went on to become a staple of school drama departments across the country, and many famous child actors such as Sarah Jessica Parker and Allison Smith took the role of Annie on Broadway. So Ashley became part of a grand history when she joined the cast of the international touring company of the much-beloved musical and went to places all over the world singing its iconic songs such as "It's the Hard-Knock Life" and "Tomorrow."

As exciting as traveling across the globe sounds, her experience with Broadway musicals also enabled her to visit the one place every kid (and a lot of grown-ups) dream about seeing up close: the White House. It was when Bill Clinton was president and Ashley was part of a troupe of young stage actors. "I was part of [The] Broadway Kids, which was a bunch of kids who were in Broadway shows, and we sang Broadway tunes and met the president," Ashley told *Newsday*. "I was so nervous, but it was really fun." From the mall in New Jersey to the White House in Washington, D.C.—all before Ashley was old enough to go to the prom. Not bad!

Around the same time as her White House performance, Ashley set her sights on another American institution: Hollywood. As much as she loved acting onstage, she no doubt aspired to get on the big screen as well. In 2001, she got an enormous break, appearing in *Donnie Darko*, a strange black comedy starring heartthrob Jake Gyllenhaal. During the filming of the movie, which would go on to become a cult classic, Ashley obviously came to understand why Jake has so many admirers. When teenhollywood.com asked Ashley who her biggest celebrity crush was, she answered, "I'd have to say Jake Gyllenhaal. I worked with him in *Donnie Darko,* so that was really cool." She gave a little bit of an embarrassed laugh during the interview that showed just how much she really meant it! So, Jake, if you're reading this . . .

Actually, at that time, the last thing Ashley had time for was a serious boyfriend, since her television career was really starting to take off.

Chapter 5

Résumé Building

By the time Ashley was a young teen, she had already proven herself to be a versatile actress who could work in a lot of different mediums. She snagged a hundred lucrative commercials. While the pay for those ads was great, she really hoped to make it doing something a little more creative, something that would really entertain people and not just sell cell phones. There was the theater. Singing and dancing were certainly not obstacles for Ashley. And she didn't lose it in front of a live audience of hundreds. And there was film. She'd had a taste of making movies with the cult classic *Donnie Darko* and a small voice role in the much-loved animated flick *A Bug's Life*. Film might be glamorous and the theater is certainly dramatic, but for Ashley, her true love was television.

Ashley's passion for the small screen began at a very young age, and she has stayed true to it for her entire career.

When a reporter from the *Miami Herald* asked Ashley in 2005 which the actress preferred, being on TV or onstage, she didn't skip a beat: "Actually, I prefer TV—even though I love theater, TV is just the best," Ashley said. "I love being on a sitcom and working in front of a live audience. I guess it's kind of like theater in that way, with an audience present, but I still absolutely love TV."

TV is tough. When you plop down on the couch to watch your favorite program, you probably have no idea of the blood, sweat, and tears that went into making it (that's a good thing, since you wouldn't be able to relax and enjoy it if you did). Television is one of the most demanding forms of popular culture. No one would say rock stars who tour all over the country, or people in the theater who go onstage night after night, don't work hard. But when compared to film, television is viewed as the grittiest, most tumultuous, generally most demanding job. Hours on a film set can be torturously long—we're talking eighteen hours a day long—but generally a movie only takes a couple of months for an actor to make. There are exceptions, but often a movie star spends a few exhausting weeks working and then returns to lounge poolside or look for the next part.

For an entire season, a television actor on a series works day in and day out, just like a person with an office job. It can take a whole week to shoot only one episode of a drama. For sitcoms, writers are often changing lines up to the last moment and even during the live-audience taping if they notice that a joke doesn't get a laugh. That requires a lot of flexibility from those who have to deliver the lines. TV actors are rewarded with about three months off during the summer. But a lot of them choose to return to work during that time, either doing plays to hone their thespian skills or auditioning for film roles in order to break into the movies (with those TV schedules, who can blame them for wanting to get into film?).

If you are on a hit show, it's still a lot of work, but it can be the greatest job in show business. That's because it is also very stable work. For a profession as volatile as acting, that means a ton. Also, people who go into acting know that part of the deal is auditioning, auditioning, auditioning, which can get really tiring. Nobody likes to be rejected, even those who are used to it.

But successful shows that run for years and years and years—such as *Friends* or *Charmed*—are one in a million. More often than not, programs are yanked before they've even had a chance to gain a loyal audience if they've gotten bad ratings during their initial episodes. It isn't uncommon to see billboards and signs across buses advertising a show that has been taken off the air so fast that the network didn't have time to stop its commercial campaign.

A lot of shows don't even make it on the air in the first place. There's a whole long process that goes into making the lineup you see on your favorite TV channel during prime time. It starts with writers and producers pitching show ideas to network executives, who usually make up their minds whether they like it or not in about sixty seconds. If the execs give the go-ahead, then the network commissions a pilot, which is a sample of the program that usually sets up the plot and relationships of the characters, which will hopefully have a chance to come alive. The networks order a bunch of these pilots, way more than would ever be able to make it on the air. Then they watch them and decide whether to order more episodes. It's a stomach-churning, nail-biting process for the producers who cook up the ideas and the actors who star in them. Ashley has had her share of disappointments when it comes to pilots. She made two that never got off the ground. One was a comedy for ABC called *The Mayor of Oyster Bay*, which was about a guy with a big ego and big dreams who becomes the mayor of a small city. Ashley also had a part in an untitled NBC pilot with Howie Mandel, the zany Canadian comedian who is famous for not liking to shake people's hands and who recently hit it big as host of the game show *Deal or No Deal*.

Ashley was certainly disappointed that neither of those pilots saw the light of day, or the light of the boob tube. But there's always more than one way to achieve a dream. In 1997, when she was only twelve years old, Ashley made her first guest appearance on a television show. She appeared on *Smart Guy*— a WB show about a genius ten-year-old tenth-grader who has problems fitting in. Ashley played a young girl named Amy in the episode that aired April 30, "A Little Knowledge," where the young genius gets into trouble when he competes on a game show called *Knowledge College*. It was only a tiny part, but it was a start.

Only six months later, her second guest appearance aired. This time it was on another WB program, the long-running classic family drama *7th Heaven,* about a reverend and his wife and all their issues raising seven children with Christian values. Ashley had the part of Janice in the episode

"Breaking Up Is Hard to Do." Landing a part on a show about the trials and tribulations of a pastor's family and friends definitely fit with Ashley's good-girl image. And to get on a show as successful as *7th Heaven* is something that any actor would kill for, since it can only help future casting directors take interest. So it seemed that Ashley's career was off and running.

Not so fast. Even the top stars have a hard time finding work in such a fickle business. Ashley was only a kid from New Jersey, just starting out. She had to continue to go on audition after audition (not to mention keep up with her schoolwork). It wasn't going to come easy. In fact, it would be a whole three years before she would land her next slew of guest appearances.

In the beginning of 2000, Ashley got a part on the iconic '90s teen drama *Beverly Hills 90210*. She played Nicole Loomis in the episode "Fertile Ground." The show was definitely winding down from its heyday when those notorious kids—Kelly, Donna, Dylan, David, Steve, Andrea, Brandon, and Brenda—and their bad behavior in limos and mansions occupied the imagination of practically every teenager in the country. Still, it was a great gig for Ashley to get. There would be plenty more that year, with appearances on *Boston Public*, *The Geena Davis Show,* and *Movie Stars*.

The parts kept on coming for Ashley. She played a runaway teen on the hit supernatural show *Charmed,* with Alyssa Milano, about three sisters who practice witchcraft. She also appeared on such popular shows as *Once and Again* and *Strong Medicine*.

Ashley was cast in shows that ran the gamut of styles and networks, from big casts to small ensembles. But Ashley was starting to get a taste for comedy by appearing on some of TV's funniest shows. The sitcom was a genre for which she would soon show a real talent. In 2002, she had a small role in the hilarious Fox comedy *Malcolm in the Middle,* about a high-school kid played by Frankie Muniz and all the trouble he gets into with his brothers. And she had another minor appearance on another funny Fox show, *Grounded for Life*, starring Donal Logue, Megyn Price, and Kevin Corrigan. She did repeat performances on *The Hughleys*, a UPN comedy about a family that moves from the inner city to the suburbs, and on *George Lopez*, the ABC family show starring the popular standup comedian.

But in 2001, Ashley finally had her goal within grasp

when she landed a regular role on a series. She was all set to play the part of Stephanie on a new Fox sitcom called *Nathan's Choice*. But this wasn't any ordinary television comedy. *Nathan's Choice*—starring J. D. Walsh and cowritten by Chuck Lorre, the cocreator and executive producer behind the popular sitcom *Dharma & Greg*—was going to be a completely interactive show where viewers decided how the plot would unfold. Sounds nuts, right? But a lot of people in the media industry were excited about this experiment. The comedy followed the life of Nathan, a recent college graduate who was totally not ready for real life. While he got into jams, viewers could use their computers or telephones to vote for one of two already-made-up story lines halfway through any given episode. (The "losing" half of the story line was supposed to run on the Fox-owned cable network FX at a later date.)

"The underlying message is that it's not always the big choices you make, but the little ones that can have unbelievable results," Lorre told *Entertainment Weekly* online in 2001, around the time of the pilot. "This is about a naïve young man who can make a lot of bad choices—and the audience is going to help him." Cool concept. But unfortunately it didn't get very far. Network executives killed *Nathan's Choice*. T. S.

Kelly, a Nielsen/NetRatings media analyst, panned the show, telling *Entertainment Weekly* online, "It's still more gimmick than substance. It'll be a test to see if content of this nature will survive." Even Lorre knew it would be hard to make into a success. "It'll be cool if it works," he said. "But it's really complicated. There's no precedent for this."

So, after seven years of acting in television, Ashley proved to be a serious small-screen veteran with twenty-one guest appearances on sixteen programs, two failed pilots, and one regular series that never got off the ground. That was quite an impressive résumé, but this hardworking actress still hadn't achieved her dream: to have a starring role on a successful television show. Many people might have given up, discouraged that despite so many opportunities, none had turned out to be the big jackpot. But, hey, this is Ashley we're talking about. There's no way she would give up on her dream so easily. And it's a good thing she didn't pack it in and return to the East Coast, because her big break was right around the corner.

Chapter 6

Too Suite for Words

Around the time Ashley was starting to wonder if her big break would ever come, the business executives at the Disney Channel—the cable network that airs live-action and animated programs aimed at younger audiences—were also looking for a hit. Not that they were strangers to success. After all, this is the station that created sensations like *Lizzie McGuire*, a popular sitcom running since 2001. But the world of television is a lot of "what have you done for me lately?"—so the executives were growing a little restless.

That's when a couple of television creators named Danny Kallis and Jim Geoghan came to them with an idea for a new live-action comedy. Their working title was *The Suite Life of Zack & Cody*. You never know what shows are going to strike a chord with audiences, so pitch meetings (that's where creative types present their ideas to the "suits" or executives) can often be fraught with suspense. Just imagine trying to sell a bunch of serious, sober businessmen and businesswomen on a show about the lives of crazy kids.

The pitch meeting for *The Suite Life of Zack & Cody* must have been a little weird because the show is about twelve-year-old twins Zack and Cody, who have just moved into a fancy hotel in Boston, Massachusetts, with their single mother, Carey, a big-time singer hired to entertain the hotel guests. As part of Carey's contract, she and her sons have been given a suite to live in on one of the hotel's upper floors. If the hotel manager, Mr. Moseby, expected Zack and Cody to behave like good little boys, was he ever mistaken. Instead, the twins turn the hotel into their own private amusement park, taking full advantage of the swimming pool, game room, and other hotel services. The result is a less than relaxing stay for many of the hotel's guests. The twins also make friends with members of the hotel staff, including Maddie, the candy-counter clerk and their sometimes babysitter.

Though the show promised plenty of hysterical hijinks, it also offered an opportunity to touch on some of the serious issues that affect children today, including divorce and moving homes. It also highlights what happens when kids end up living in a world that includes a lot of room service. That's probably why the Disney executives went for *The Suite Life*. "It gives you back of the house/front of the house," Danny Kallis, one of the show's cocreators, told the *New York Times*. "It gives you blue-collar/white-collar. It gives you the high life, when you can't really afford it."

Once Disney gave *The Suite Life* the green light, it was time to think about assembling the crew. They brought in two talented veteran directors named Henry Chan and Richard Correll. Then the casting agents got down to filling the various parts. The lead roles of Zack and Cody were practically written for real-life twin sensations Cole and Dylan Sprouse—but more on them later.

Casting the supporting parts proved a little trickier. That's often the case with television and movies because creators will often have a certain actor in mind for the lead role when they are writing a script, so they really tailor it to his or her particular strengths. The supporting parts are usually not very clearly defined, so it is harder to find the perfect actors for them. The upside to this is that it allows the actor who gets the part to really own the character and make it his or her own.

Casting agents will pore through hundreds of "head shots" (pictures of actors, along with biographical data and work history), looking for actors who might be right for the part. It can be a pretty random process, actually. Fortunately, because Ashley had worked so hard, appearing in over a hundred commercials and taking small parts here and there in other television shows and even a few movies, her face was familiar to a lot of agents. At some point, the *Suite Life* producers decided to call her in for an audition, though for what part exactly, they couldn't say. "I did a couple of pilots for a network series and finally went for a Disney pilot," Ashley told thestarscoop.com. "I went in and actually tested for both roles, London and Maddie."

Now that audiences know Ashley as the sweet-natured and sensible candy-counter clerk, Maddie, it's almost impossible to imagine her playing London, the spoiled and self-centered daughter of the hotel owner. But the casting agents obviously saw in Ashley a versatile actress who could play either part (and, given the next big role she would land in *High School Musical*, can you fault them?). In the end, though, good triumphed over evil and Ashley was awarded the part of Maddie—much to her relief, as it turned out.

Ashley wanted the audience to love her before they would love to hate her, as they would when she played Sharpay in *High School Musical*. "I'm really glad that I ended up with Maddie, because for fans to first get to know me, I'd rather them look up to this character who is more like me, rather than Sharpay," she told thestarscoop.com. Brenda Song, the beautiful actress who got the role of snooty London Tipton, had already been on Disney for a long time, so Ashley explained, "It's easier to see that she's not like that."

The part was right, the setting was right, and even the network was right. In fact, Ashley was absolutely thrilled to be acting on the Disney Channel. The channel is known as a family network, which refers mainly to the type of wholesome shows it airs (no violence or foul language there, thank you very much). But it also describes the community of actors it has fostered over the years. In a way, being on a show that airs on the Disney Channel is like being initiated into an exclusive club. Think of all the super-talented stars who got their start at Disney—from Britney Spears to Justin Timberlake to Hilary Duff, and more.

Ashley also didn't have to worry about not knowing anyone when she showed up at the Disney studios. She was already friends with Raven-Symone Pearman, the star of the Disney show *That's So Raven*, as well as the gorgeous sisters and talented musical duo Alyson Renae "Aly" and Amanda Joy "AJ" Michalka. Aly, a star on the hit Disney series *Phil of the Future*, was also the star of the channel's original movie *Now You See It*. The sisters, who have written and performed music for some of their shows, costar in the Disney TV series *Haversham Hall*.

"It's fate that I ended up there," Ashley said to thestarscoop.com. "I've known Raven since I was three. I hadn't seen her for the longest time! Now I'm in the same hallway as her. It's crazy. I've known Aly and AJ since they were really little. We were in acting class together." And, as if that weren't enough, Ashley had even met her costar Brenda. "I've known Brenda since I did a Bette Midler show," Ashley said. "Once you're in the business, you just kind of get to know everybody. You audition with these people, you're friends with these people. I always stay friends with everybody."

Not that it would be all fun and relaxation. As Ashley had already learned, working in television is a tough life. That's true even if you get to be on a show with a lot of close friends. Even if the executives at the Disney Channel create a nice environment for their actors, they still want their programs to succeed and make money for the company. That translates into plenty of hard work and long hours.Fortunately, Ashley had the experience of her childhood to draw on, in particular the lessons her father had taught her about the meaning of an honest day's labor. With that and all the love both parents had given her, she was confident that she would rise to the challenge of *The Suite Life*. Now, she was just excited to get started.

Chapter 7

Home Away from Home: Life on *The Suite Life*

T he first day on the set of a new show can be a lot like the first day of school. Everybody is usually super-excited but also a little on the nervous side. After all, for every new series that goes on to become a huge, gigantic hit, there are dozens that end up getting panned by the critics and yanked from the lineup. And it's almost impossible to predict the winners from the losers. (Otherwise, do you think the big-shot executives would waste their money making flops!?)

Besides being worried that their show might bomb, actors also fret over whether or not they'll get along with the rest of the cast. The entertainment industry is full of stories of television shows and big-screen movies failing because of a lack of chemistry between their actors.

If Ashley had any of these fears or reservations that first day of shooting *The Suite Life*, she sure didn't show it. In fact, she told *Popstar!* magazine that the first day on set was "exciting and happy." But then, unlike many actors in similar situations, she had plenty to be excited and happy about.

For one thing, she was pretty confident that *The Suite Life* was going to succeed. Her reason? Well, she had two, actually: Their names were Cole and Dylan Sprouse. Television has no shortage of pint-sized superstars (just check out the careers of Mary-Kate and Ashley Olsen), but even with so many accomplished child stars coming before them, there was something extra-special about the Sprouses.

The twins were born fifteen minutes apart (Dylan is older), on August 4, 1992, in Arezzo, Italy. Their parents must have suspected that their boys were bound for fame, since they named them after stars: Cole for the famous jazz singer Nat King Cole, and Dylan after the lionized Irish poet, Dylan Thomas.

After their family returned to Southern California from Europe, the twins waited all of six months before starting their careers in front of the camera. Their first gig was a commercial selling toilet paper! They obviously had star quality, because right away they were tapped to play Brett Butler's youngest child, Patrick Kelly, on the hit ABC series *Grace Under Fire* (like the Olsen twins, they often shared the same part).

The stellar job they did on that show led to other television appearances, including *Friends*, where they played the son of Ross (David Schwimmer).

Though the Sprouses worked steadily throughout most of the '90s, their true breakout moment didn't come until 1999, when they appeared opposite Adam Sandler in the smash-hit movie *Big Daddy*. That's where audiences got their first true taste of the irresistible Sprouses. Among their newest and most ardent admirers was none other than Ashley Tisdale. "When *Big Daddy* came out, I fell in love with the boys and told my mom I was going to work with them someday," Ashley recalled in an interview with *Popstar!* magazine. "When I found out they were in [*The Suite Life*], I freaked out and said, 'I have to get this job!' "

Being able to work with the Sprouses was probably the best thing about Ashley's new job, but it wasn't the only thing. She would also be reunited with one of her closest friends in the industry: Brenda Song, who plays the part of London, the spoiled and sometimes spiteful daughter of the hotel owner. Though Brenda is a few years younger than Ashley (she was born on March 27, 1988), the two actresses are the closest of friends. "Brenda and I are like sisters," Ashley told *American*

Cheerleader magazine. "I knew her for four years before the show even started. It's the coolest thing to get to work with my best friend."

So, between the Sprouse twins and Brenda Song, Ashley was pretty psyched about her new cast mates. But not even she was prepared for how totally sweet life on *The Suite Life* would be. Of course, the days are long, just like they are on the set of any television show. But, like the saying goes: "Time flies when you're having fun"—so it hardly felt like work for Ashley and company. "It's so great," Ashley said to KriSeLen.com. "We all work really hard, but when we have lunch breaks, Brenda and I are always getting our nails done or going shopping. Everyone's a huge family. It's great to get to work with people you love."

The family comparison is repeated by just about everyone involved in the making of *The Suite Life*, and that definitely contributes to its success. As any actor will tell you, the best shows are the ones where the cast gets along well and genuinely enjoys coming to work. And it doesn't hurt having a couple of pranksters like Cody and Dylan on hand to provide occasional comic relief. "They're so funny and normal, like boys," Ashley said on mediavillage.com. "They play nonstop.

They just don't care. That's the best part about them." Despite their flair for hijinks, the Sprouses are also respectful of their coworkers, which Ashley attributes to positive upbringing (something else she can relate to). "Their dad has really kept them grounded," she told mediavillage.com. "When they're off from work they're hanging out with their friends and not doing events and stuff. That's really refreshing."

The Sprouses obviously think highly of their coworkers as well, especially Ashley and Brenda, whom they seem to view almost like big sisters. "They're really, really nice," Cole offered in an article for *Tiger Beat* magazine. "I've met some celebrities that are pretty mean. Ashley and Brenda are just naturally cool." That's high praise coming from a boy.

Even though the Sprouses are quite a bit younger than Ashley, their praise must feel pretty good. After all, they are the stars of *The Suite Life*, which was apparent from day one of the filming (not that the twins ever hold it over people's heads; they really are as humble as they come). The title characters, Zack and Cody, were created specifically with Dylan and Cole in mind. "[The Disney creators] asked us what type of show we would want if we had our own show," explained Dylan to *Popstar!* magazine in 2005. "The writers spent a lot of time getting to know us, so our characters are based on what we're like in real life."

The Zack/Dylan character is more of a mischief-maker. He's not that interested in school, and he would much rather spend the afternoon playing video games and getting up to no good. The Cody/Cole character, on the other hand, is sweet and innocent and a terrific student. He's often the unwitting accomplice to his brother's pranks, getting sucked into the shenanigans without even realizing it.

Though these parts were pretty clearly defined, the supporting cast of characters took some time to flesh out. As we already know, Ashley actually tried out for the parts of Maddie *and* London. She was relieved to get the part of the candy-counter clerk because it's similar to how she is in real life. "She is a lot like me. I love her style. She's a little bit more sarcastic than I am," Ashley said, describing Maddie to *Scholastic News* online. "She's a funny girl and always getting into trouble with London, but she always knows how to get out of it; she's a really smart girl and I love portraying someone who is really smart."

Despite the similarities, it still took Ashley a little while to grow into the part. As with any acting role, hair and makeup was a big help, literally transforming Ashley into Maddie. A new hairdo was part of the reinvention, according to Ozlem Dalgic, one of the show's lead stylists. "We lightened [Ashley's] basic hair color to a light beige-blond and then highlighted throughout," she told *Sophisticate's Hairstyle*. "The character Maddie is very smart, but fun and kind of quirky and spunky! I think her hairstyle suits that character in the fact that it's so textured. It's a very fun cut but, at the same time, it's a very smart cut."

The new coif definitely helped Ashley get into character. From there, it was just a matter of practicing her lines and letting herself become Maddie. Actors have all sorts of tricks that help them prepare for a part. They often draw from real-life experiences. For instance, though Ashley never worked as a candy-counter clerk, she did have a job at the mall when she was growing up. No doubt, the experience of dealing with the occasionally snooty customer gave her some good insights into what it might be like to work in a fancy hotel.

After a few weeks of rehearsal Mondays through Fridays, things really started to click for Ashley and the cast. They often perform in front of a live studio audience, which many actors find energizing (as opposed to just performing for the camera). Ashley, always the cheerleader, is responsible for warming up the crowd. "Every morning on show days I always do the welcome speech," she told *American Cheerleader* magazine. "I do this whole speech with so much energy, and then, at the very end, I do a high kick. When you bring lots of energy to things, everyone just becomes more happy."

Her energy definitely did the trick. The show premiered on March 18, 2005, with the episode titled "Hotel Hangout." In that first show, Zack and Cody make friends with Max and Tapeworm, while Maddie develops a crush on Lance, the hotel lifeguard. The episode had its share of pranks, laughs, and even a few semi-serious moments. It really set the tone for the season, and audiences were almost immediately hooked.

Every show that followed was equally anticipated by the growing legion of fans. Though it's hard for Ashley to single out her one favorite episode, she clearly enjoyed some more than others. "I loved 'Rockstar in the House,' with Jesse McCartney," she said to *Scholastic News* online about working with the pop-star sensation who also happens to be a hottie. "He is so cute. It was such a great episode and so much fun to do. There was so much for me, London, and Zack to do. It was really cool and a great experience working with Jesse."

As *The Suite Life* started to generate a larger and larger following, Ashley got her first taste of true celebrity (and the riches that come with it). She splurged on a new car and clothes, though she's always been careful about not going overboard with the material possessions. She also started to develop a real fan base. At first, it was a little strange to be spotted in public, but Ashley got used to it soon enough. One afternoon she entered a local restaurant and ". . . ten little girls at dinner for a birthday started screaming when I walked in," she said with a smile in an interview for missoandfriends.com.

Ashley also experienced the buzz and excitement of mixing with other stars. "I'm a huge fan of Brittany Murphy," she confided to *American Cheerleader* magazine. "I saw her at the Nickelodeon Kids' Choice Awards and went up to her, not knowing what she'd be like, and she was the nicest person! She talked to me for, like, twenty minutes and told me to never give up on my dreams."

All in all, things were looking pretty good for Ashley. As she said to *Sophisticate's Hairstyle*, "I'm so happy with *The Suite Life*. I just believe this is where I'm supposed to be because I'm the happiest." As happy as Ashley was, it was probably impossible for her to imagine life getting any better.

But something was about to happen that promised to blow
everything else out of the water.

Chapter 8

High School Musical: Here We Come!

Musicals are about as American as the Stars and Stripes or apple pie. But they're not always considered the height of cool. How many of your friends have show tunes from *Oklahoma!* or *The Sound of Music* piping through their iPods? Every now and then, though, a musical comes along that really shakes up the genre. In the 1970s there was *Grease*, a coming-of-age saga about a good girl who falls for a bad boy with slicked-back hair and a leather jacket. Then in the 1980s there was *Flashdance*, which told the story of a Philadelphia welder who aspired to be a ballerina. In the 1990s, audiences went wild for *Rent*, the stage sensation that put lyrics to bohemian life in New York City.

But the current generation didn't have its trailblazing musical to gyrate to. Always on the lookout for cultural holes in need of filling, the creative executives at Disney sensed an opportunity. They pulled together some of the most talented people in the industry to whip up a story. We don't have to tell you what the talent came back with. *High School Musical* is without a doubt one of the hugest song-and-dance extravaganzas of the new millennium.

Like most successful creations, the story line to *High School Musical* is pretty simple. The romantic comedy takes place at East High, a fictitious school located in Albuquerque, New Mexico. The action revolves around the unlikely relationship that bubbles up between BMOC (that's big man on campus) Troy Bolton and the shy, studious Gabriella Montez after they perform a duet at a local karaoke contest during the winter vacation. When they realize they attend the same high school, they decide to pursue their passion for singing together and try out for the leads in the musical.

That's where it would have ended happily ever after, except for one small problem: teen drama queen Sharpay Evans. Along with her brother, Ryan, Sharpay has starred in her school's musicals for the past ten years (since kindergarten!) and she's not about to surrender the spotlight to a couple of amateur upstarts. Making matters worse for Troy and Gabriella, Troy's basketball teammates and Gabriella's fellow scholastic decathletes have their own reasons to want the budding courtship to crash and burn. But in the end, love—and music—conquers all, and Troy and Gabriella win the leads in the musical, not to mention each other's hearts and the admiration of their peers.

   High School Musical is a classic boy-meets-girl story, and that's probably why it has struck a cord with fans. It is the kind of movie that all audiences can relate to—female and male, young kids and older ones—which was very much the plan all along. "I wanted to make a film that didn't speak down to anyone," the film's producer, Bill Borden, told the *Florida Sun-Sentinel*. In so doing, he looked to the timeless love stories for inspiration. "I drew from a lot of things. I love Franco Zeffirelli's *Romeo and Juliet*. That was one of my biggest influences, seeing that when I was a freshman in high school. The whole balcony scene in [*High School Musical*] was influenced by that."

   It may sound strange to hear that *High School Musical* was influenced by a play written by William Shakespeare, but if you know your Elizabethan theater, you know that the Bard (as Shakespeare was commonly called) was writing for the masses, not just the noble classes. The creative team behind *High School Musical* also wanted to generate widespread appeal.

Injecting lots of singing and dancing into the script seemed like a surefire way to crank up the energy and enthusiasm.

Given that the action takes place in a high school with hundreds of students, this made for some fairly complicated scenes. So Disney brought an accomplished director-choreographer named Danny Ortega on board to execute the production. He had already directed and choreographed the made-for-Disney movie *Newsies*, so the company executives knew they were getting a reliable professional. But, more importantly, Ortega had quality experience overseeing large dance scenes. For instance, he was the lead choreographer on the wildly popular movie *Dirty Dancing*, which starred Patrick Swayze as a dance instructor at a summer camp retreat. Ortega also choreographed the big-production parade scene from the school-cutting classic *Ferris Bueller's Day Off*, which involved hundreds of extras winding their way through the streets of Chicago. Clearly, this guy had the chops to take on *High School Musical*.

Ortega already had a script to work with, which was written by Peter Barsocchini, whose past credits included *Shadow-Ops* and *Drop Zone*. Barsocchini had delivered a strong story, but what the production really needed was some show-stopping musical numbers. Rather than rely on one songwriter, Ortega and producer Bill Borden decided to assemble several pop songwriting teams. The teams were chosen for their distinctive styles, which explains the wonderful range of sounds in the movie, from cute and catchy to slow and sentimental. The songwriters were also very adept at incorporating exact lines from Barsocchini's script into the lyrics, so the singing scenes and regular speaking ones blend together seamlessly.

With the script in place and the musical numbers just in need of some fine-tuning, the production team was able to turn its attention to finding a place to shoot the movie. After scouting several locations throughout the American Southwest, they settled on Salt Lake City, Utah. It looked enough like Albuquerque, New Mexico (where the action is supposed to take place), plus, Ortega knew the city well from the work he had done there for the 2002 Winter Olympics.

They were ready to go! Well, almost. There was just one final matter: casting the movie. A few hundred miles away, Ashley Tisdale was wrapping up another season of *The Suite Life*, wondering how on earth she was going to spend her twelve-week break from the show.

Chapter 9
Drama Queen

The *Suite Life of Zack & Cody*, like most shows on television, is shot one season at a time. Let's say there are twenty-five episodes in a season. The actors and crew will spend about six months filming those shows, then take a few months off. Most actors relish their vacation time. But like you already know, Ashley Tisdale isn't like most actors. As a result, she wasn't much looking forward to her time away from the set of *The Suite Life*.

"I literally went on hiatus for [*The*] *Suite Life* last summer," she told thestarscoop.com. "I love working. When I'm not working, I get so bored. I was, like, what am I going to do for, like, a couple of months? I don't know what I'm going to do. So for two weeks on hiatus, I was already bored. I was, like, I need to do something."

Fortunately for Ashley, the casting agents hired for *High School Musical* were gearing up for their next assignment. They knew they wanted some fresh faces to appear in the movie, so they sent out a casting call that literally anyone could respond to. Hundreds of actors did, so the competition for the main roles was really intense.

But Ashley had one advantage: The movie's producer, Bill Borden, was already familiar with her work. "I didn't know any of these kids except for Ashley Tisdale," he told the *Florida Sun-Sentinel*. "I knew her from the Disney show [*The Suite Life of Zack & Cody*]." Clearly, all the hard work she put in was starting to pay off. But that doesn't mean parts were just being handed to her. She had to prove there was a role right for her in *this* film.

"Suddenly, *High School Musical* came around and I went to audition for it," she said to thestarscoop.com. "It wasn't given to me. A lot of people think it is because I'm on Disney, but I had to go on the audition, and to the callback. It wasn't like it was handed to me at all. I had to go in there and get it myself."

Besides her vast television experience, the fact that Ashley toured with the Broadway musical *Les Misérables* also impressed the production team. They definitely wanted her to be in the movie, but for which part? Given how likable Ashley's character Maddie is on *The Suite Life,* she probably figured she'd be a shoo-in for the part of Gabriella, the brainy Goody Two-shoes. So it must have been a huge surprise when the producers called to tell her that she'd been awarded the role of Sharpay, the popular It girl who rules the school.

What a departure this would be from her character of Maddie! But Ashley wasn't complaining. After all, the more characters an actress plays, the better she becomes at capturing different attitudes and emotions. Ashley really understood this. "[The characters] are totally different," she said on thestarscoop.com. "Maddie's, like, this girl next door, she's really, really smart, she gets along with everybody. She's always doing something crazy or insane. She's really sweet, and Sharpay is just the total opposite. She's the most popular girl, she dresses like she's going to a red-carpet event. It's funny because she's mean, but she always has a smile on. But they're totally different."

To help get into the character of Sharpay, Ashley watched a bunch of films that featured equally mean-spirited characters. "I watched a lot of movies to prepare for playing her," she told mediavillage.com. "I actually watched *Mean Girls*, with Rachel McAdams, and I liked how she portrayed her character. She was a mean girl, but she had a smile on her face whenever she did it. So I watched all these other things and kind of put some things in and made it creative myself. I just loved playing the mean girl." Ashley actually found that she liked acting like someone totally different than herself. It was a surprise. "I love playing the drama queen," she admitted to the *Asbury Park Press*. "Because that's so not like who I am."

Ashley may not be a drama queen in real life, but with her career taking off into the stratosphere, she was looking more and more like the queen of drama. That's especially true compared to her fellow cast mates, who were all relatively unknown. Ashley quickly emerged as the seasoned veteran on staff, the actress whom the others would look up to the most.

Of all the actors, the one who was probably the greenest was Zac Efron, who landed the part of jock-turned-thespian Troy Bolton. Though Zac played the part of Cameron Bale on the television show *Summerland*, he never considered himself a serious actor. "At this point, when people ask me if I'm an actor, I say I'm a student," Zac told *Teen People*. "Acting has always been a hobby. It's just now that my hobby is taking off. My friends finally get to see what I've been doing all these years." Zac may have been nonchalant about his acting talents, but his looks definitely put him in the star zone. Everyone could see that he is a total hottie!

So if acting was merely a hobby for Zac, dancing was something he'd never even contemplated. "It was tough," he said on *Showbiz Tonight*. "I had no dance experience. I wasn't ready. It was tough, man, it was very tough." And as if *that* wasn't enough, Zac even had to bone up on his basketball skills. "I am *not* a basketball player," he admitted. "I had one real season under my belt, playing with kids who were so much better than me, it was embarrassing. I think I scored two points all season. So it took a lot of practice, to say the least."

The rest of the lead actors were a little better off than Zac. There was Vanessa Anne Hudgens, who played the part of Gabriella. Vanessa was already a member of the Disney family, having acted in the action adventure *Thunderbirds*. For her, starring in *High School Musical* was a dream come true, since it was a chance to dust off her dancing shoes. "I grew up in San Diego, but I'm originally from Oregon," she told *Scholastic News* online. "I'm from a really small town with one stoplight. I used to sing and dance around the house. But there weren't enough people for a dance class. So we moved to California."

Like Ashley, Vanessa has the benefit of positive role models in her mother and father. "My parents have done so much for me," she said. "I started doing singing and dancing in theater and my friend asked me to go on an audition for a commercial, and ever since then I knew I wanted to do this."

Vanessa was actually homeschooled, so unlike her fellow actors, she didn't have real-life experience to draw on with regard to what life in a high school is like. But she adapted well, so much so that her role in *High School Musical* had all the makings of a breakout performance (and, in fact, she appeared in *The Suite Life* alongside Ashley since filming the movie). If Ashley was missing her pal Brenda Song from *The Suite Life*, Vanessa provided a good stand-in. "She is one of my best friends," Ashley told *Tiger Beat* magazine, "which is funny 'cause I'm so mean to her in the movie."

When they weren't filming, Ashley and Vanessa would often squeeze in a few hours of shopping for clothes, having lunch, or hanging out with the other cast members, including Lucas Grabeel, who played Sharpay's brother and coconspirator. Lucas had been working hard in Hollywood since moving there in 2003, after graduating from high school in Springfield, Missouri. He landed the part after impressing producer Bill Borden during the casting call. "He did this little song-and-dance number and had so much personality, I was immediately attracted to him to play this role in our movie," Borden told the *Springfield News-Leader*. At age twenty-one, Lucas was actually the oldest of the movie's main characters, though he had no trouble getting goofy. "I'm committed to getting a laugh," he told the *Atlanta Journal-Constitution*.

The other two actors who rounded out Ashley's posse on set were Monique Coleman, who played math whiz Taylor McKessie, and Corbin Bleu, the Brooklyn, New York—born star of the hit television show *Flight 29 Down* (with the unforgettable head of hair) who handled the part of Chad Danforth, Troy's teammate on the basketball team.

Though the main members of the cast came from different places, they all clicked pretty much immediately. For Ashley, who was used to the strong, family vibe from *The Suite Life*, it was great to work again with such cool people who got along so well. "It was so much fun and it seems like just yesterday that we did it," she told tommy2.net in 2006. "But ya know, it was a blast and we had so much fun during the whole thing. Everybody is, like, ya know, it's like another family besides *Suite Life*. We just kind of bonded and I have all these new friends and we're really excited to see everybody's reaction 'cause for us it's really cool."

Of course, the making of *High School Musical* wasn't just hanging out and having fun. The entire production had to be shot in twenty-five days on a five-million-dollar budget. If that sounds like a lot of money, just think: Some blockbusters can cost around two hundred million dollars and take over a year to make.

Fortunately, the cast had a steady leader in the director, Kenny Ortega. He had worked with even tighter budgets and shooting schedules, so he knew what had to happen to get the movie made. "Our director was amazing to work with," Ashley told KriSeLen.com. "We had a two-week boot camp where we danced from nine in the morning until six o'clock. We also recorded all our music prior to going to Utah, where we shot the movie, and laid down seven tracks in five days, which is amazing because it usually takes more than that."

Some of the actors fared better at boot camp than others. Zac Efron, who's actually had the theme to *Rocky* as his cell phone ring tone, didn't exactly handle it like a champ. "It was Broadway style," he said, describing the regimen to *Scholastic News* online. "We'd wake up at six in the morning and work until six at night. It was a very long day, but by the end, I'd sustained so many injuries and was so sore but so much better than I was before. I learned more in those two weeks than I'd learned in the previous years."

Besides the benefit of learning, Zac also had the comfort of enjoying the company of his cast mates . . . a lot! "That was one of the benefits of being in this movie," he told teenhollywood.com. "Lots of pretty girls." Though there weren't any on-set romances (or so he says!), Zac will admit that "[the cast] immediately became best friends. We got a good group, which is very rare. There wasn't a bad seed among any of the kids."

Once filming began, the cast settled into a regular routine, though Ashley admits that life on a movie set is quite different from what she was used to on *The Suite Life*. "With a sitcom, you have a live audience," she told mediavillage.com. "We go in, we rehearse, we're done by four or done by three, and everything moves quickly. With a movie, they have to get all different shots. You block and then you film it, so it takes a lot of patience. It's a very cool experience."

Despite the endless rehearsals (or maybe because of them!) the set of *High School Musical* had its share of bloopers and practical jokes. "It was like a party every day for us," Ashley told *Tiger Beat* magazine. As for the flubbed lines, everyone seemed to have their own embarrassing story to tell. "I really hope that [they show] the bloopers!" Vanessa Anne Hudgens said to tommy2.net. "'Cause we had some funny bloopers, I must say. Like Zac had one where he was, like, trying to put his shirt on but he couldn't and he took it off and ran back and forth and, like, it was hysterical. So I hope we have bloopers."

But for all the fun and games that they had, the cast members were also working hard, in part because there was a growing sense on set that the movie had something special to it. "There were moments," Monique Coleman, who played Taylor McKessie, told *Showbiz Tonight*. "There were little glimmers shooting a couple of scenes that there's something special going here, specifically the final scene."

Besides the growing optimism that spurred the actors to push themselves harder and harder, filming a movie is just plain difficult. As glamorous as the lifestyle may seem, the days are long and actors are often forced to do difficult things. Ashley, for instance, who loves to walk around in sandals, had trouble adjusting to her character Sharpay's preferred footwear. "I never really liked high heels and I was really scared because she wore high heels all the time," she told teenhollywood.com. That made for some tricky dance numbers, especially "Bop to the Top," which took a full day to get just right (and the song is only a few minutes long!).

Then, of course, there was the scene where Sharpay gets food dumped on her in the cafeteria. Nobody likes that! "It was horrible!" Ashley complained to teenhollywood.com. "It was chili and it smelled so bad. The worst part was that I had to take a shower in the boys' locker room—the *real* boys' locker room." Yuck!

It certainly was an adventurous twenty-five days of filming for the cast and crew of *High School Musical*. But they got the job done and made a few new friends in the process. For Ashley, it was the perfect way to spend her time off between seasons of *The Suite Life*. She probably left Utah for her life back in California thinking that the experience of *High School Musical* was pretty much behind her. Little did she know that the show had only just begun!

Chapter 10
Straight to the Head of the Class

High School Musical had its premiere on January 20, 2006. That was a Friday night, which meant that the movie went up against a lot of other programs targeted at younger audiences. After all, the television executives in charge of scheduling knew that after the long school week, kids love to get together with friends for a few hours of Friday night entertainment. So High School Musical definitely wasn't the only teen-friendly program on the tube that night.

While networks always hope that a new show will attract more viewers than expected, they try to keep their expectations to a minimum. That included the executives at Disney, who went about their weekend like normal, thinking as little about High School Musical as about their own high-school experiences from years ago.

But when they walked into their offices on Monday morning, they were treated to quite a pleasant surprise. Their little movie about life as a teenage thespian had scored huge ratings, attracting over seven million viewers! That was a record for the network and good enough to make *High School Musical* the top-rated, non-sports cable broadcast for the month. It would also go on to earn the highest rating of all movies that ran on cable television in January 2006. You can just imagine the men and women in business suits doing high fives all around as these record-setting numbers rolled in. "We never planned on this," Gary Marsh, president of entertainment for Disney Channel Worldwide, told the *Chicago Sun-Times*. "This movie has taken on a life of its own."

Meanwhile, in schools all across the country, the buzz over *High School Musical* was catching on like wildfire. In the hallways and cafeterias, during homeroom and throughout recess, it was all the kids could talk about. "How cute is Zac?" they gushed, many of them making comparisons to their own high-school hotties. "Sharpay is such a snob! She got what she deserved," others declared, probably drawing worried looks from any It-girl peers within earshot.

The fact that there are so many characters in *High School Musical* that kids can relate to is definitely one reason for the movie's success. "I think these characters are really relatable,"

Ashley told *Showbiz Tonight*. "You've gone to school with our characters. I think they're a little bit exaggerated. But, you know, everyone has a Sharpay and everyone has a brainy girl. It's just actually, like, you relate to it, especially adults do." Chris Byrne, a children's marketing expert, seconded the idea that *High School Musical* is for kids of all ages (and maybe a few adults thrown in). "It's inspirational for younger kids because it's about people they look up to," he told the *Chicago Sun-Times*. "Yet older kids have tuned in because it reflects their social world, touching on what it means to be a stranger."

It's true that beyond the catchy show tunes and scintillating dance scenes, *High School Musical* is very much a story with strong values. The fact that Troy and Gabriella follow their hearts and aren't swayed by peer pressure delivers a really positive message to real kids who might find themselves in similar predicaments. All the actors involved agreed, including Ashley. "The whole movie is about being true to yourself and not being in a clique," she explained to *Scholastic News* online. "You don't have to just be one thing. Kids can get stuck in a clique and can't get out of it. You feel that people won't support you in anything else. I think it's important to find yourself in school and be happy about it. And if people don't support you, they're not your real friends."

Believe it or not, the idea that kids at school can make you feel insecure is something even Ashley has experience with. Even though she would probably be the coolest student at any school, Ashley explained how close to home the movie hit for her. "When I was in school, I kind of went through the same thing," she said on *Good Morning America*. "There's all these cliques and it's really important because everyone can relate, I mean, even older adults can relate because you know these characters so well in our movie. And you know, it's like stepping out of that clique, and feeling like you can say what you are, what else you want to do, and not find yourself after school but [during] school. I think that's really important for kids to learn that. I think it's really amazing. It's a good message."

Zac Efron, who played the part of Troy Bolton in *High School Musical*, views his character's transformation in the movie as ultimately inspirational. "The message from the movie is that you have to be yourself, walk your own path," he told *Scholastic News* online. "Don't listen to all the pressures that come from the outside world. Troy starts out as this hotshot stud, but he's given that name by his peers—it's not really who he is. By the end of the movie, he discovers he can be himself and have just as much fun. He goes through this great transformation. By the end of the movie, he's even cooler." Well said, Zac!

Okay, so everyone thinks the same thing: *High School Musical* has a strong message. Nobody's denying that. But let's face it, there are other reasons the movie developed such a devoted and ever-expanding audience in a relatively short span of time. Consider this: During the six airings between January 20 and February 12, 2006, 26.3 million new viewers tuned in to see this movie! This strategy of repeatedly airing the movie, and gaining a larger audience every time, is new for the entertainment industry. "We live in a culture where it's all about the big opening weekend and nothing else," Chris Byrne said in the *Chicago Sun-Times*. "That isn't what happened here, though. They've allowed it to build slowly by word of mouth, and quite frankly I think it's in a much stronger position as a result." You're not the only one, Chris!

No doubt, *High School Musical* scored big with audiences, but the buzz must have been about more than the movie's positive message and strong core values. So what was it? Well, for one thing, the movie had a terrific sound track. That's something the Disney executives were well aware of even before the movie aired. A few weeks prior to its premiere, they released many of the songs online and offered free downloads of the single, "Breaking Free." Then, just one week ahead of the premiere date, they released the sound track in stores and started showing music videos from the movie on the Disney Channel. That was enough to catch a lot of teenage ears, so the movie had a pretty good-sized fan base to build on even before it hit the small screen.

The early promotions really paid off. In the weeks following the premiere of *High School Musical,* nine songs from the sound track appeared on the Billboard Hot 100 (that's the music industry's weekly list of most-listened-to songs). Just imagine how psyched the cast of *High School Musical* was to see their names next to mega pop stars like Beyoncé, Nelly, and Kelly Clarkson. Or to learn that the band The B5s had done a version of the single "Get'cha Head in the Game," and that the NBA had picked it up as one of its promotional tunes. Slam dunk!

Of all the songs on the sound track, "Breaking Free," the movie's anthem, has probably enjoyed the most success.

In one week it jumped from number 86 to number 4—that's the fastest one-week jump in *Billboard* history! According to Geoff Mayfield, *Billboard* magazine's director of charts and senior analyst, the sound track to *High School Musical* was the surprise hit of 2006. "Album sales have grown every week it's been on the market," he told the *Chicago Sun-Times*. "Even weeks in which it wasn't number one, it still sold more than the prior week. No one saw it coming."

It's not surprising that "Breaking Free" is the most popular song on the sound track, since it really sums up *High School Musical* as a whole. The duet is sung by Zac Efron (Troy) and Vanessa Anne Hudgens (Gabriella), and it's all about how they will achieve their goals if they remain true to their hearts. Another favorite hit is "Stick to the Status Quo," which touches on a similar theme of the perils of peer pressure. Its words are so inspirational that they actually cause one of Troy's sports teammates to admit he loves to bake and aspires only to make the perfect crème brûlée!

Obviously, Disney had met its goal of making a musical that younger audiences would find cool. For Ashley, who was no stranger to stardom after the success of *The Suite Life*, it was an enormous thrill to be a part of such a tremendous cultural event. "The movie's pretty much like *Grease* for our generation," she told *American Cheerleader* magazine. "We sing and dance and break out in song. . . . It's so much fun."

Back in California, Ashley couldn't believe the attention *High School Musical* was receiving—not that she was complaining! "It's crazy. It's, like, it's huge," she told tommy2.net. "I mean, we never expected this much. We knew the movie was gonna be really good 'cause we all can feel that. And we knew it was gonna be fun, and kids would like it. But I think the album coming out of left field and going gold is, like, absolutely nuts. We never imagined that in a million years." Ashley couldn't have been happier. The world realized what she, her costars, and producers knew. She couldn't have summed up the experience any better than when she said, "It's really, really awesome!"

Ashley's other cast mates were just as excited (and surprised) by how well *High School Musical* was doing. "You know it's phenomenal," Vanessa told tommy2.net. "I mean, we knew it was going to be a big thing, but nobody knew it was going to be this big." For the girl from a one-stoplight town in Oregon, the feeling was extraordinary. "Of course I'm just so proud, and it's so great hearing me on the radio. It's phenomenal, really."

Ashley Tisdale

Red-carpet ready!

Dancing the night away
in *High School Musical*

Ashley
performing
one of her
hit songs
for fans

𝓐shley and Brenda Song are even better friends than their characters, Maddie and London, on *The Suite Life of Zack & Cody*.

𝓐shley poses with her sister, Jennifer, and a friend at a Nickelodeon screening.

Ashley
looking
sweet!

Though Ashley's acting abilities are what landed her the role in *High School Musical*, she's a big part of the success of the sound track. She had already proved her singing chops by performing Broadway musicals for a bunch of years, and now with the sound track, she's thrilled that her talents are reaching a wider audience. It's been quite the breakout moment. In fact, Ashley is one of the only female artists ever to have two songs debut in the same week on the Billboard Hot 100. Needless to say, she's had to pinch herself more than a few times. "I have to say, the weirdest thing was looking at the *Billboard* charts and seeing, like, Beyoncé and Sean Paul and all these people and then seeing Ashley Tisdale. I was, like, *no way!*" she told tommy2.net. "That was just the weirdest thing ever. It was really cool, it was a dream come true because I really wanted to record and do an album one day."

The two songs that launched Ashley to the top of the charts were "What I've Been Looking For" and "Bop to the Top." She performed both tunes with Lucas Grabeel, who played her brother Ryan in the film. Lucas—who moved to Los Angeles from St. Louis, Missouri, in order to make it in show business—was as blown away by his good fortune as everyone else involved in *High School Musical*. He told tommy2.net, "You know the album going gold and all these kids just going crazy and all the iTunes downloads and everything, it's insane."

To get a sense of just how insane it all is, consider this: Even tracks that didn't make it into the movie are turning into hit songs on the radio and online. Case in point: "I Can't Take My Eyes off of You," another one of Ashley's recordings. "It was an additional song written by Matthew Gerrard, who did 'We're All in This Together' [and other songs in the movie]," she explained to mediavillage.com. "He had pitched the song and we knew we weren't going to use it, but we just recorded it, anyway." It's a pretty good sign when even the rejects from a sound track turn into pop favorites, though there's a small part of Ashley that wishes otherwise. "It's kind of weird because it's me and Lucas," she said about doing a strange love-duet with the actor who plays her younger brother, Ryan. "My kid brother is singing it with me and I'm singing 'I can't take my eyes off of you.' But it's a really nice song. It's not really our characters singing."

Though Ashley obviously loves the limelight, her single favorite moment from the filming of *High School Musical* was one she shared with literally hundreds of other performers. "I would have to say [that] the musical number [at the end of the movie] was my favorite because it was so amazing and there were so many people," she said. "There were, like, three hundred extras. It was an amazing feeling. It was the best way to end it and it was like a big party. We were just told to have fun and be happy, and that's just how it turned out."

That sounds like the perfect end to a totally perfect movie experience—lots of people together having fun and being happy. And the number of viewers who are getting in on the good feeling of *High School Musical* continues to get larger every day. The result has been even greater fame and celebrity for Ashley. She gets recognized practically everywhere she goes nowadays. And people constantly approach her for autographs and pictures. "Yeah, they know me as Ashley because [Disney] kind of promotes my name," she told thestarscoop.com. "I just went to a Cheetah Girls concert and I could not believe how many people [were there] . . . I got mobbed. It was unreal. In the amphitheater, they were chanting 'Ashley.' I thought Ashlee Simpson was there, and it was actually me."

Sitting in that stadium with thousands of fans chanting her name, life was pretty sweet for Ashley Tisdale. From that moment in the mall seventeen years ago when she was first discovered through a few star turns on the stage to a leading role on a hit television show and now a starring part in the biggest movie in cable history, her career has only known one direction: up. She may not be quite as big as Ashlee Simpson—not just yet, anyhow. But, everyone knows, it's just a matter of time.

You probably think that with all her newfound fame and celebrity, Ashley has started taking limousines everywhere and eating only at five-star restaurants. But, in fact, she has remained more Maddie than Sharpay. Life may never be "normal" for a mega star, but for Ashley, it's pretty close.

Chapter 11

Keeping It Real

Ashley's just like any regular girl. Yeah, right. Okay, so she's not completely ordinary, but when she wakes up, the first thing she does in the morning is brush her teeth. Well, that's normal, anyway. Seriously, though, now that you have heard all about the fabulous career of Ms. Tisdale the Star, what's it like during a typical day in the life of Ashley?

The first thing to know is that almost immediately after brushing her teeth, she needs a caffeine blast. Ashley's not really awake until she hits her local java outpost of the California coffee chain, Coffee Bean. There, she downs a large vanilla ice blend. It's healthy, though—the tasty concoction is blended with ice and nonfat milk.

Ashley does have to think about fitting into all the latest clothes and looking great on camera (which makes people look a lot bigger than they are), but that doesn't keep her from eating. The Disney star isn't one of those emaciated celebrities who gets filled up by the smell of food. No, Ashley enjoys a good meal. One of her favorite foods is sushi—pretty sophisticated fare. Raw fish isn't everybody's idea of a tasty treat, but in L.A., where Ashley lives, it is as popular as pizza.

Speaking of pizza . . . while Ashley may love fancy food, like sushi, she isn't too good for ordinary junk food, such as gooey, cheesy pizza, which she loves. But out of all the taco shacks, sandwich shops, and other fast-food joints in California, her favorite is the drive-through burger stand In-N-Out Burger. The West Coast chain is not only Ashley's favorite. Loads of other celebrities (and regular people) are crazy for the burgers. There's even a secret In-N-Out menu, for those in the know, including Animal Style (a burger with the works), Protein Style (a burger wrapped in lettuce), or 4X4 (four patties and four slices of cheese stacked between the bun!). Ashley's meal of choice is a hamburger with french fries topped off by a thick chocolate shake.

With all the pressure on young women in Hollywood, Ashley does have to watch her weight. But she has a healthy approach to the whole process. Instead of forsaking food, she eats in moderation and works out to keep her supercute figure. Ashley's routine is to exercise with a professional trainer three times a week. A lot of celebrities use trainers to make the most out of their time at the gym. It's a great way to really make the muscles ripple, if you can afford a trainer's fees.

Ashley doesn't just care for her body. If you are a star, you have to work on just about every aspect of your appearance. But Ashley takes meticulous care of her hair. That's totally understandable—since those long blond tresses are part of her trademark look. But we already know the big secret: Ashley's natural hair is not straight at all. She's got a head full of curls! But she never, ever wears her hair curly, opting instead to straighten it. That can be really hard on the hair's texture. So Ashley has to take extreme measures to make sure she doesn't fry her glossy mane.

"Ashley takes really good care of her hair," her personal and show hairstylist Ozlem Dalgic assured *Sophisticate's Hairstyle* in 2005. "She's really careful about trying to keep her hair in the best condition possible. Using the best products shampoo and conditioner-wise will definitely give you the optimum result when straightening thick, curly hair like that." And that's not all. Ashley keeps a tight lock on split ends. "She gets trims about once every eight to ten weeks and we do deep conditioners at least once a week," Dalgic revealed.

That's a lot of maintenance. Between beauty rituals and learning her lines, how does Ashley find any time to kick back? Recently she moved out of her parents' house in Valencia, California, and into her own condo, which she purchased. That can be a pretty traumatic time for anyone, especially for someone as close to her family as Ashley is. But not only did her best friend and dog move in with her, she didn't move all that far from her family, or from a home-cooked meal. "My parents are just down the block," Ashley told *People* magazine in 2006. "So we'll be eating at their house!"

Still, Ashley is psyched about her new pad. She told the website missoandfriends.com that her house "is the best place to relax." On her days off, Ashley could do anything she wants, but she loves to stay at home and watch movies. Instead of hitting the hottest clubs or restaurants all night, Ashley thinks a great evening is one where she pops in a favorite film and kicks back with a couple of friends. Ashley is nuts for chick flicks, especially ones with marriage themes. Some of her favorites are *Just Married* and *My Best Friend's Wedding*. Hmmm . . . is Ashley dreaming about heading down the aisle? Maybe, but right now she's content to be in the company of her pals, lounging around and watching teen TV on her big screen.

When Ashley isn't checking out her own work on the Disney Channel, she loves to watch MTV, especially *Laguna Beach,* a show that follows the wild lives of eight real teens who live in Orange County, California. "I'm addicted to *Laguna Beach,*" she told *American Cheerleader.* "I really love that show."

Don't get the wrong idea. Ashley's not a total TV junkie. Even though she's on it and loves to watch it, she does make time for that good ol' fashioned hobby: reading. Her life is crazy busy, but she curls up with a book whenever she can. "I do like to read. I think it's really important," Ashley told *Scholastic News* online. "It's awesome because it relaxes you. You just put yourself into that book and pretend you're that person in that experience. I read anywhere I can. I love to read in the car. When I'm rehearsing and working, I love to go into my dressing room and read."

Believe it or not, another thing Ashley likes to do during her downtime is something she does for a living. "Singing is something I have always loved to do, so in my downtime I always go back to that," Ashley told the *Miami Herald* in 2005. She also admits to a secret addiction, something you would never expect: knitting! It's much cooler than it seems. Knitting isn't just for grannies anymore. It's become a popular trend among stars such as Julia Roberts and Cameron Diaz. It makes sense that people with lives as insane as celebrities would enjoy a slow activity like knitting. It's also a good way to pass all the downtime on set. Anyway, how cool would it be to get a scarf knit by Ashley?

Ashley has a full life, her own apartment, an amazing job, and great friends. She's pretty much a full-fledged grown-up. But that doesn't mean she can't miss her parents. She does. To make her house seem homier, without her tight-knit clan, she cribs from her mom's recipes. For dinner she told missoandfriends.com, "I try to make my mom's homemade Caesar salad." Hmmm, that doesn't sound too convincing. She also relishes the holidays when they all get together. "I love Christmas, not just because of the presents but because of all the decorations and lights and the warmth of the season," Ashley said on her website, ashleytisdale.com. Her pet dog is never left out of the plans. She is crazy for Blondie, her Maltipoo. "She is sooooo cute!" Ashley squealed to missoandfriends.com.

At heart, Ashley is basically just a big kid. Maybe that's why she conquers her fear of flying by taking either her mother or a stuffed animal (but preferably both) on any plane she boards. Maybe that's also the secret to her success in staying so grounded despite the rush of fame she's experienced. The spring of 2006 brought a flurry of attention. She landed in the pages and on the covers of *Teen* magazine, *People*, *Popstar!*, *Tiger Beat,* and *Bop*. Not to mention all the premieres, parties, and free clothes. "I'm really having the time of my life," Ashley told the *Asbury Park Press*. "Sometimes it's hard to believe it's happening to me." It would be easy for Ashley to forget where she came from and become a major snob. She has people calling out her name wherever she goes. But fame hasn't changed Ashley at all. "It's kind of crazy but I feel no different than I did before I landed my first job," she told teenhollywood.com "I'm still me. I think I'll always be grounded because my parents keep me that way."

One person who isn't ashamed to flaunt Ashley's fame is her grandmother, Marilyn Morris. Ashley and her grandma, who lives in Ocean Township, New Jersey, are really tight. And Marilyn likes to brag about her granddaughter's phenomenal success. She tells all her friends, "I'm Maddie's grandmother." And now, since *High School Musical* has become a hit, she's switched her refrain to "Sharpay's grandmother." The whole thing makes Ashley laugh. "She's been really supportive of everything I've done," Ashley said. "She's really one of my biggest fans."

But don't think her parents, Lisa and Mike, are joining the Ashley cheering squad. Their job is to keep her the sweet daughter they raised. "It's never going to go to my head," Ashley said about her fame to the *Asbury Park Press* in 2006. "My mom would smack me if I ever started acting the diva."

Chapter 12

Future Tense

With such a charmed past and present, it's pretty clear that Ashley has a bright future ahead of her. The success of *High School Musical* is steamrolling ahead. The film pulled in millions of viewers every time it aired on the Disney Channel. With that momentum, the much-anticipated DVD of *High School Musical* arrived in stores May 23, 2006. Who would think that people would want to see Ashley's flick after it repeated on TV about nine times? But they did. Maybe it's because the DVD came in two versions: the original, and a sing-along edition that has lyrics at the bottom of the screen for fans who don't already know every word from watching it a million times. How many karaoke sessions did that spawn?

Vanessa Anne Hudgens loved watching the extra scenes on the DVD, but they did remind her of how much pain those red shoes she wore in the film caused her. "I actually watched the behind-the-scenes version today and I was, like, 'Oh, my God, what was I doing?'" she told teenhollywood.com. "It hurt, but I somehow made it through. I walked in London for miles with these stiletto boots and I survived, so I guess I'm really good with heels."

It's lucky Vanessa has a way with heels because she might just have to put them back on, since a sequel to *High School Musical* is in the works. With the success of the first one, it was inevitable. Producers are smart people who like to make the most out of a good thing. Ashley and Zac couldn't be more excited about the project. They were the first actors to sign on to *High School Musical 2*.

It isn't surprising that Ashley jumped on the opportunity. She's savvy. But when will she find time to fit it all in? Ashley is a hot actress who is totally in demand. She picked up a recurring role in *Kim Possible*, an animated series by—surprise, surprise—Disney about an ordinary high-school student who saves the world after class. And of course there's her role as Maddie in the next season of *The Suite Life,* which starts shooting in the spring.

But Ashley wouldn't let a little thing like scheduling keep her from a part in a big movie. She's got it all planned out. When the second season of *The Suite Life* wraps in October, she has a lot of goals to accomplish—the *High School Musical* sequel, maybe another movie, and what about a concert? Nothing is out of her grasp. Despite all her big dreams, Ashley is still firmly grounded in her Disney sitcom. She wouldn't want anything to get in the way of that right now, or, as she told teenhollywood.com, "I don't want to say good-bye to that yet!"

One thing she would love to do but hasn't yet had a chance to make happen is a project with her sister Jennifer, who is also an actress. "I would love to work with her," she told the *Miami Herald* in 2005. "We did a commercial together, and I would love to maybe have her on the TV show or even do a movie with her. I know it would be fun." Older sis Jennifer is absolutely gorgeous, just like Ashley. Some families have all the luck. While Ashley has a cute, girl-next-door look, Jennifer is the sexy, unapproachable type with very blond hair, very high heels, and very dark eye makeup.

Maybe her vampy look is the reason Jennifer has landed so many parts in seriously scary horror films. She also made a guest appearance on one TV show, *Boston Public*, a Fox drama about the ups and downs of teaching at a high school in Boston. Created by David E. Kelley, the Emmy Award—winning force behind *Ally McBeal* and *The Practice*, *Boston Public* had a long run (for TV, that is), from 2000 to 2004.

Alas, Jennifer only made it on one episode of the drama, but she seems to have more of a knack for the horror genre. In the past four years she's appeared in three gruesome films, starting with *Ted Bundy* in 2002. That was a docudrama— a film that's kind of like a documentary in style and research— based on the real life of Ted Bundy, a notorious serial killer who murdered at least nineteen young women during the 1970s. The film follows Bundy from his college years through mass murder on to his trial. Next up on Jennifer's tour of terror was a part in the 2004 film *The Hillside Strangler*. The title pretty much sums up the entire plot of this slasher film. Just when you thought things couldn't get any darker for fair Jennifer, she landed a part in the 2005 film *Dark Ride,* about a killer who escapes from a mental institution and goes to, where else, a theme park. Sounds like fun. The horror film, which literally had people on the Internet movie sites warning innocent audience members of the freakish violence, also starred Jamie-Lynn DiScala, who became famous playing mob princess Meadow on the HBO gangster hit *The Sopranos*.

Screaming in the woods and running away from

psycho killers—those parts Jennifer played are a far cry from the sweet, wholesome Disney roles Ashley lands. So perhaps before the Tisdale sisters can share a trailer on a TV or movie project, Jennifer may have to lay off the gore.

All this talk about work, work, work. What about extracurricular activities, such as, well, boys? Doesn't a little fun lie in Ashley's future? When it comes to her love life, Ashley keeps her cards really close to her chest. You'll never see paparazzi pictures or read tabloid items about her canoodling with some guy in a club. Everyone wants to see Ashley in love. So much so that the press and various fan sites had her dating her costar, the hunky Zac Efron. Who wouldn't want to date him? Despite the rumor mill and Zac's obvious appeal, the two are not seeing each other. So what is Ashley looking for in a guy? "I look for someone who's really fun to be with. Someone you feel comfortable with and have a good time [with]. Tall, surfer," she joked with teenhollywood.com in 2006. "It's mainly about the personality, though."

Whatever guy she ends up with, Ashley certainly won't rely on him for financial support. This is a girl who loves to work. Luckily she's had tremendous success in the field of her choice. But Ashley says that if she couldn't be in the entertainment industry, she'd be a writer. "I have always wanted to do this my whole life, but I also love to write," she told KriSeLen.com. "I love to write music, scripts, anything! So I probably would be a writer."

Well, Ashley can put the pen and paper away for now. Her acting career is red hot. Ashley's set to take over the entire entertainment industry. She told KriSeLen.com that in five years, she'd like to be "in a TV show still and doing movies, maybe performing in concerts with an album!"

Music has always been a big part of Ashley's life, first through her stint with live theater and then, of course, with her big breakout hit *High School Musical*. Never content to rest on her past achievements, Ashley wants to push the music thing even further by making an album of her very own. Certainly the *High School Musical* CD proved that she has the goods. Ashley has five amazing songs on the *Billboard* charts. "Hopefully it's leading up to recording a CD one day," she told *Scholastic News* online. "I love to write music, and I've been writing a lot of stuff." A lot of stuff is right. Ashley has actually been writing her butt off. That "someday" for the release of her CD might be sooner than you think. "I just wrote twelve songs and am putting together a demo to see who is interested in producing [it for] me," she told the *Miami Herald*. So keep your eyes on those CD racks for an Ashley Tisdale album!

Ashley already has designs on duets with two top singers. "I would love to do a duet with Jessica Simpson. She's a great singer. And Jesse McCartney one day," she told teenpeople.com. Jessica Simpson is actually Ashley's personal role model. Although Ashley is surrounded by famous people almost every day of her life, she is completely starstruck by Jessica. "I think I'd pass out if I met her," Ashley told *People* in 2006. Really, the two girls aren't that far apart. They both are blond. They both can sing, dance, and act. And they both have pet Maltipoos—a breed of dog that's a mix of a Maltese and a poodle—(Jessica's is called Daisy). But while Jessica is on the cover of practically every big gossip magazine almost every week, Ashley is more subdued. "I'm more like the girl next door," she told teenhollywood.com in 2006.

No matter what her other aspirations are, TV remains her first and foremost passion. Being a television star is a dream she's still working on. "*High School Musical* was the first real movie I really did," she told thestarscoop.com. "So I definitely want to do more movies. But I always, always want to have a sitcom. I would love to always have a TV show and then do movies on the side as well. . . . I love TV. My goal is to win an Emmy one day, not an Oscar."

And just as Ashley dreams big for herself, so does she encourage others. Her message has always remained the same. "Don't ever give up," she advised her fans in an interview with the *Miami Herald*. "It is important to pursue your dreams. Don't let anyone, or any rejection, keep you from what you want. Always stick to your goals." Spoken like a true star.

Chapter 13

Ashley's Style File

Now that Ashley has become a superstar, lots of girls her age and younger have had a chance to check out her style. The jury is in: They definitely like what they see. That's because Ashley not only knows how to bend the best of current trends to flatter her own look, she's also a trendsetter herself. With her flowing, fancy tank tops, long hair, chunky jewelry, and cool jeans, she is the epitome of current young fashion. Ashley's hip but not too mature, pairing designer items with everyday mall purchases. *The Suite Life* star takes a nod from one of her personal heroes and style icon Jessica Simpson. "I would take a picture with Jessica Simpson because I love her style!" she told missoandfriends.com. Just like Jessica, Ashley is equally comfortable in a pair of cool sweats and oversized shades, or a girly dress and leather clutch.

Ashley's style is so awesome that it has even influenced the stylists of *The Suite Life* and *High School Musical* when they created her characters' wardrobes. "Maddie is very casual and comfy," Ashley told the *New York Times* in 2006. "Sharpay was way over the top and bedazzled. Her style was based on my Sidekick cell phone, which is pink and sparkly. I'm a mix of both because I love to wear Uggs and leggings and be casual, but I also like dressing up." Well, no wonder the costume designers followed her lead. Now with a few insider tips, you can become a little more like Ashley.

It All Starts with the Outfit

Ashley knows that in order to look good, you have to be the entire package (including a nice person). But like building a house, you must start with a strong foundation. For Ashley, that's the clothes. "I always pick my wardrobe first. Once I have that, I do my hair and then match my makeup," she told *Sophisticate's Hairstyle* in 2005. She doesn't discriminate when it comes to designers, shopping the entire spectrum of cool clothes. Some of her favorite lines include Diesel, BeBe, Urban Outfitters, Betsey Johnson, Abercrombie & Fitch, and Hollister. "My wardrobe stylist on [*The*] *Suite Life* puts all my stuff together from Forever 21," she told teenhollywood.com in

2006. "I love Diesel and I love Urban Outfitters. I just go and look and buy things if I like them."

At this point in her life, Ashley can buy anything that catches her eye because she is a big star with a big bank account. But that wasn't always true, even though she did always love to shop. Ashley never let a lack of funds stand in the way of fashion. She found a way to make money for her shopping habit at a very early age by working in retail while she was growing up. She even worked at the supercute and preppy store Abercrombie & Fitch. "It wasn't fun," Ashley admitted to *People* in 2006. "But I did love getting a discount. Everything I earned went back to whatever store I was working in!"

TiP: A solid wardrobe of high-quality items is the base for any kind of stylish person. No matter how cute your haircut or earrings are, if you pair it with a boring T-shirt and jeans, they will get lost. Shop around for the looks that best suit your body and personality (and, if you're breaking Mom and Dad's bank, use Ashley's example and get a job!).

Don't Be Afraid to Experiment

Ashley is relaxed in everything she does, including her style. "I like to wear sweats and cute T-shirts. Sometimes if I'm going out, I'll wear jeans and a cute top," she told *Sophisticate's Hairstyle*. No ball gown there. In fact, Ashley confided to missoandfriends.com that her coolest article of clothing is "my Juicy Couture sweats that have 'Heiress' written all over them." Juicy Couture is practically required wearing in L.A., where every starlet and starlet-wannabe walks around in the matching tight sweats, clutching a big cup of Starbucks. But recently, Ashley has been taking more risks with her style, having discovered such edgy independent designers as Ed Hardy. And her risks are paying off. "Lately, I've been wearing pinstriped shorts over leggings and I just bought a wide belt that comes up under my chest," Ashley told the *New York Times*. Well, that's one outfit that would certainly get attention.

TiP: Once you've mastered the basics, experiment a little. Having good style isn't just about looking perfect. It's about creating an individual look that gets attention. If something out of the ordinary catches your eye, try it on and take a chance.

A Perfect Head of Hair

Ashley has naturally curly hair but always wears it pin straight. That takes a lot of work. Ashley's personal and professional hairstylist, Ozlem Dalgic, goes through a long process almost every day to create that seemingly natural and effortless look. "We always blow-dry her hair. Then we flat-iron it to give a little bit of extra shine and smoothness," Ozlem told *Sophisticate's Hairstyle*. It's really important to use high-quality brushes, irons, dryers, and products if you are going to put your hair through so many processes. "I do most of the straightening with the bigger round brush. I really do my best to take small sections and get the root of the hair as straight as possible by pulling it with my fingers," Ozlem revealed. "Then I use the straight iron only from the middle of the shaft on down to the ends." Ozlem's last touch is to smooth a little pomade onto Ashley's hair so that no frizzies ever get a chance to pop up. If that sounds like a lot of work, it is. Ozlem gets paid a salary just to tend to Ashley's hair. Nobody, except a star or a zillionaire, can afford that kind of personal attention on their hair. And to do it yourself would take forever. (No matter how much you love style, there are some things more important than spending hours on your hair, like sleeping or eating . . .)

TiP: There are a few shortcuts you can take to get glossy hair à la Ashley. Wash your hair in the evening and use a deep conditioner. Blow-dry it straight and follow up with a pomade or straightening serum. Then sleep on it. Your hair will flatten during the night, mimicking the process of a straightening iron. If you have really curly hair, don't go for the completely straight look. Make braids while the hair is still wet and dry for loose, tousled waves.

Heat's a Killer

Applying high heat on a regular basis can really damage hair. Frequent straightening makes products more important than ever. With Ashley's regimen of intense heat and drying to kill those curls, her products need to hydrate, hydrate, hydrate. "Deep conditioning is essential because I have naturally curly hair and straighten it a lot, so I have to deep condition [it] a lot—otherwise, it's just going to die!" Ashley told *Popstar!* magazine in 2005. To keep Ashley's locks healthy, Ozlem uses PureOlogy Hydrate Shampoo and Hydrate Conditioner. "To protect Ashley's hair and add a lot of shine, I use Schwarzkopf Osis Magic Anti-Frizz Serum," Ozlem added.

Long, Short, Pink, or Blond: Try It All

Everyone knows Ashley as a beautiful blonde on camera. But on her own time, she's a little more adventurous with her hair. She isn't afraid to experiment with different colors just as long as she's ready to be a sweet blonde again when the cameras roll. She's able to do that by using hair extensions—fake hair that is woven into your real hair. The extensions are ideal for actresses because they can come in or out in a jiffy. That's why you see stars with short hair one day and completely long hair the next. Britney Spears is a huge fan of hair extensions. You never know what length her locks will be on any given day.

"Once in a while, depending on what she's wearing and the vibe of it all, Ashley likes to put in different colored

extensions," Ozlem told *Sophisticate's Hairstyle*. "We just
did a couple of pieces of pink on either side of her hair and it
looked fabulous against the blond!"

TiP: It's fun to play around with non-permanent
hair dyes to create new and individual looks or to match
an incredible outfit. Save up and splurge on hair extensions
for a super-special occasion like the prom. Your date will
definitely be surprised and psyched when, instead of
your usual bob, you have a waist-length mane.

Accessorize, Accessorize, Accessorize

Ashley knows the value of a good accessory. Even her
technology is accessorized: In addition to her Motorola Razr
cell phone, she carries around a Juicy Couture Sidekick from
T-Mobile. That must look hot with her Juicy sweat suit. But
Ashley also knows her limits. While her *High School Musical*
costar Vanessa Anne Hudgens may be a pro in tall stilettos,
Ashley can't stand spiky heels. "I'm horrible in heels," she told
Sophisticate's Hairstyle. "I have to wear flats. I have the cutest
ballerina slippers for dressy events." Whatever it is—jewelry,

bags, shoes—Ashley chooses carefully, often splurging on one big-ticket item instead of a lot of lame stuff. She did just that when she bought a Louis Vuitton Globe Shopper Cabas tote (which almost resembles a shopping bag with writing all over it) that she told the *New York Times* was her "first really major handbag purchase." Now that's a huge purchase. But find your own limit.

> **TiP:** Save up for one special item as opposed to spending a little money on lots of little junky items. If it's truly a classy purse or pair of shoes, it will make many different outfits look a whole lot better.

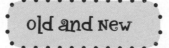

old and new

You can't get much more current than Ashley's style (Juicy Sidekick, hello!). Still, she doesn't discard things that are old. She told missoandfriends.com that her most prized possession is "a charm bracelet from my grandma." Sentimental items are the best, better than the latest hottest trend. Ashley believes that. She wears a Me&Ro leather string bracelet that is a keepsake from *High School Musical*. We already know dreams are important to Ashley, but they even factor into her outfit with a favorite cuff by Dillon Rogers, which reads: "Follow Your Dreams."

TiP: Take a second look at jewelry and other items that come from close friends and family. Although on first inspection they might not seem "stylish," their meaning and the love they come with will transcend any trend.

Chapter 14

Lucky Stars

Ashley Tisdale is certainly poised to give young teen stars like Hilary Duff and Lindsay Lohan a run for their money when it comes to being Hollywood's newest sweetheart, but Ashley is anything but a diva. She could easily be the girl next door or your new best friend, and she has the star sign to prove it! Ashley was born on July 2, which means she's a sweet-natured Cancer. Cancers are known for their patient, gentle personalities and their tenacity and sharpened survival instincts, so it's a safe bet that Ashley will be around for a long time to come.

Cancer is one of the three water signs (along with Scorpio and Pisces) and, like all water signs, Cancers have deeply developed instincts, intuition, and feelings. Cancer's lucky colors, sea green and silver, and precious stone, the pearl, come from the ocean, and, just like the tides, Cancer is ruled by the moon. Water signs know to trust their gut when it comes to making decisions, and they have been known to relax or become stressed based simply on "a feeling" they have about a situation or event. Ashley knows to rely on her superstrong intuition, and it hasn't failed her yet. Basing her career moves on her instincts about certain parts have led her to portray characters suitable for her age and personality instead of rushing into racier and edgier roles like some of the other Hollywood starlets her age. Ashley has been more comfortable establishing herself as a talented, wholesome young actress and easing into more mature roles—and so far, it's working. After all, whether she's playing a lovable sweetheart or the girl you love to hate, Ashley is irresistible!

Cancers have a bad reputation for being crabby and moody, thanks to the ocean dweller that symbolizes this sign: the crab. Ashley is as far from crabby as you can get, but she does share some of the crab's more lovable qualities. Crabs have hard shells that protect them from predators, and Ashley has developed a thick skin of her own in the years she's been working in showbiz. Auditioning for part after part means a lot of rejection, but Ashley has a hard shell of dreams and a firm belief in herself to get her through all the "nos." Like most Cancers, Ashley is very driven and always has her mind on the future and what she wants to accomplish. Being super-dedicated to her goals and dreams means that Ashley always has something to strive for and look forward to, giving her the discipline to keep working hard even when it isn't easy. The crab's hard shell is part of the reason that crabs have been around for over five hundred million years, and tenacity like Ashley's means she'll probably outlast a lot of other stars her age. She's a survivor, and that's just fine with us—we can't wait to see her in future roles!

Underneath that hard shell, Cancers are very sensitive and loving. They are family oriented and treat their friends like an extension of their family. Ashley is certainly close to hers—she moved out to be on her own, but only a few blocks away! And that's far enough for her for now. Cancers like the feeling of being safe and protected with the people they love. They also tend to prefer to stay home and relax instead of going out partying all night. Ashley's favorite way to unwind with her friends is to kick back at home with a movie and yummy snacks, in true Cancer fashion. Ashley and her sister are the best of friends, and she'll never pass up one of their mom's home-cooked meals. But Ashley has created family for herself outside of the family she was born into. Working on *The Suite*

Life of Zack & Cody has given Ashley a new sister in Brenda Song and little brothers in Dylan and Cole Sprouse. Ashley loves taking care of her friends and costars and, like all Cancers, she is very nurturing. She's the first to offer a hug when someone is having a bad day or make someone who's sad smile with her goofy antics. And, of course, Ashley uses her Cancer intuition to give great advice to her friends and family, just like other famous Crabs—"Dear Abby" and the Dalai Lama!

Cancers tend to be shy and sensitive, and Ashley wasn't always the outgoing sparkler we know and love today. She credits cheerleading with helping her get over her shy nature—but we think she was just born a star! Because Cancers can be sensitive and get their feelings hurt easily, they are always careful to be mindful of others' feelings and like to make sure that everyone is happy and having fun. Cancers often get a bad rap for having mood swings, but smart Cancers like Ashley know that this can work to their advantage. They feel things deeply and know their emotions in and out. Ashley is able to channel this into her acting. She can portray emotions realistically because she feels everything so deeply.

Cancers are also known for being great comedians and performers once they come out of their shells—which explains why Ashley has such a gift for comedy. Ashley even uses her childhood clumsiness to help her fall naturally when performing physical comedy. Cancers have sharp minds and great memories, and Ashley is no exception. Her fantastic memory helps her memorize lines and dance numbers quickly. She can even play a song on the piano after hearing it only once—talk about talent! Ashley is also extremely smart and hard-working, pushing herself relentlessly to achieve her dreams. That's one powerful combination: talent and drive— no wonder she's such a success!

When it comes to love, Cancers are very picky. They prefer a mate to be one of the other water signs, like a fellow Cancer or a Scorpio or a Pisces. Cancers need someone sensitive and stable who will make an effort to get under their shell and truly understand them. Aries can be too harsh for Cancers, and Aquarius is too wishy-washy, making either a bad match. Cancers like Ashley tend to take their time finding the right person, but when they do, it's often an intense and long-lasting bond.

Ashley hasn't been linked romantically with any Hollywood hotties yet, but when she finds the right guy, we'll know because she won't be able to keep her happiness from showing. Cancers long for true love and never give up hope of finding their soul mates, even if they don't talk about it openly. Once in love, Cancers are fiercely loyal and protective, providing their mate with security and comfort. Cancers are often private about their deepest desires and most personal feelings, choosing to protect and nourish them until the perfect moment. This tendency means that people are often surprised by Cancer's accomplishments because they don't see them coming until the last minute.

Ashley, like the crab symbol of her star sign, is one tenacious chick. She's smart and intuitive and never gives up on the things she truly wants and works for. She plays up her strengths and has learned how to turn her weaknesses into helpful qualities—channeling her sensitive emotions into her acting abilities and her stubbornness into an unstoppable work ethic. Ashley would clearly go far no matter which sign she was born under, but her Cancer instincts and drive to survive certainly help. It's her Cancer sweetness, loyalty, and kindness that have made her into the Hollywood sweetheart we just can't stop watching!

Chapter 15

By the Numbers

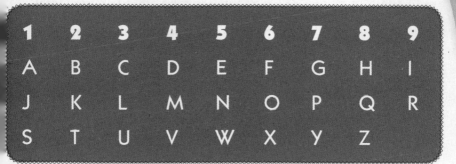

1	2	3	4	5	6	7	8	9
A	B	C	D	E	F	G	H	I
J	K	L	M	N	O	P	Q	R
S	T	U	V	W	X	Y	Z	

Ever wonder what gives a celebrity that elusive star quality? The answer could be in his or her name—and it can be found using numerology. Numerology has been practiced by mathematicians since Galileo's time and it's still used today by celebrities and nonstars alike, to determine how their name can affect who they are.

Numerology uses the relationship between the letters in a person's name to determine specific characteristics of that person's personality. Each letter in the name is matched up with a particular number from a numerology chart. The numbers are then added up to reveal that person's master number. For example, Ashley's full name is Ashley Michelle Tisdale. By matching the numbers from the numerology chart to the letters in her name, "Ashley" is 25 or can be read as 7 (25 is broken down to 2 plus 5). "Michelle" is 40 or 4, and "Tisdale" is 25 or 7. The numbers are then added and the total is 18, which can then be broken down to the single digit of 9. This 9 reveals the truth behind Ashley's beautiful name. As a 9, Ashley is intuitive, creative, a born businesswoman, and a dreamer—with an amazing ability to see the big picture and to become a leader in her community.

It's easy to see why Ashley is a 9! Her career as an actress has been fueled by her creativity and intuition for choosing just the right roles. As a 9, she knows to trust her instincts, and it's clear she does. Sure of how she'd like her career to progress, Ashley accepts only roles that she feels will propel her in that direction. She's held on to her good-girl image by choosing roles—such as Maddie on *The Suite Life of Zack & Cody*—that are close to her own personality. But now that Ashley has established herself, she's beginning to branch out into more demanding roles. In *High School Musical*, she played Sharpay, the popular and mean drama queen—quite a stretch for sweet Ashley! She embraced this role because it was different from anything she had done before. She was ready for the challenge.

Ashley is a born businesswoman, but her "business" is her acting career, which she handles like a pro. Ashley has resisted the temptation to give in to the Hollywood pressure that says she must look like every other waif actress onscreen. She hasn't embraced a racier, more sexual image because that isn't who she is or wants to be. Ashley knows that trends come and go, so she strives to be a classic performer—one who can handle any part and isn't stereotyped into one specific type of role. Ashley is an exception in young Hollywood, taking only roles that she thinks will give her career staying power and momentum. As a 9, Ashley is always looking at the bigger picture. She avoids shock-value parts and chooses roles with substance instead. She doesn't want just her fifteen minutes of fame . . . she's planning on fifteen years of fame—or longer!

As a 9, Ashley seeks to improve the world around her. One of the reasons she's been eager to portray "good-girl" characters is to be a positive role model for her fans. Ashley attended regular school growing up, missing only a few days at a time to film commercials, so she knows what it's like to deal with peer pressure, growing pains, and finding your own identity. Ashley loves playing Maddie on *The Suite Life* because Maddie is a lot like her—an average girl who is a good friend, a hard worker, and who always tries to do the right thing in every situation. Maddie also attempts to teach London, the snobby heiress character on the show, how to become a better friend and a less selfish person. Fans of the show have an excellent role model in Maddie, and in Ashley. Ashley goes out of her way to attend many Disney events so she can interact with her fans and encourage them in person. And she chooses to dress stylishly in an age-appropriate way, even when she isn't on TV or making an official appearance—to help young girls realize that you don't have to wear too-tight clothes or show skin to be pretty. In a pop-culture-saturated world that encourages girls to grow up too fast, girl-next-door Ashley is a breath of fresh air for her fans.

Sometimes, 9's can be accused of not paying enough attention to details, but, while Ashley has a tendency to focus more on the bigger picture, life's little details don't escape her! Ashley handles finances with finesse, making smart purchases such as a condo and a car, instead of blowing all of her money on lavish parties or a closet full of designer duds. Ashley is always stylin', of course, but she does it on a budget—picking up her clothes at less expensive stores like BeBe and Abercrombie & Fitch, instead of high-end designer shops.

When it comes to style, Ashley is all about the details. You'll never catch her out and about without serious accessories. She loves to complete her look with the perfect bag or pair of shoes. She doesn't go overboard with baubles, but what she does choose makes a statement. How else could she appear on so many Best-Dressed lists? And you have to be patient and pay close attention to details with a beauty regimen like Ashley's. Ashley's naturally dark, coarse, curly hair has to be deep-conditioned, straightened, highlighted, and infused with lots of beauty products to keep it looking so luscious. Ashley has perfected her overall look by planning down to the tiniest details, which is pretty sweet!

Ashley is definitely a 9 when it comes to being a dreamer. She knew what she wanted from an early age and never gave up on her dream of becoming a star. She's worked tirelessly on multiple commercials, television appearances, and guest roles to get where she is today—and she couldn't have done any of that if she didn't have a clear vision of her dream to keep her motivated. Ashley believed in her dream so much that she bargained with her parents to give her a year to pursue acting full-time. If she didn't make it, she said, she'd then go to college and choose another career. Ashley knew that she had what it takes to succeed. She wasn't going to let anyone—even her parents—keep her from going for it. Now that she's finally a small-screen star, her dreams can only get bigger and better, which means we can expect plenty more from Ashley in the future.

Numerology isn't an exact science, but it can often provide valuable clues about people's strengths, weaknesses, and overall personalities. In Ashley's case—with her creativity, intuitive nature, and business smarts—numerology shows that she was born to be a star. But it was Ashley herself who made her dreams come true. Numerology just gives us a better picture of the girl behind all the glamour.

Chapter 16

Are You an Ashley Expert?

How well do you know Ashley Tisdale? Take this quiz to find out!

1. Where was Ashley discovered?

2. When is Ashley's birthday?

3. Where was Ashley born?

4. What was Ashley's first acting gig?

5. What is the name of Ashley's character on *The Suite Life of Zack & Cody*?

6. What is the name of Ashley's dog?

7. What is Ashley's zodiac sign?

8. What was Ashley's character's name in *High School Musical*?

9. In what show did Ashley make her Broadway debut?

10. What was Ashley's favorite class in school?

11. What is Ashley's favorite color?

12. What is the food Ashley can't live without?

13. Who is Ashley's favorite actress?

14. On *The Suite Life of Zack & Cody,* Ashley plays a candy-counter clerk, but what was Ashley's real life high-school job?

15. What is Ashley's favorite TV show?

16. What top actress did Ashley work with in a T-Mobile commercial?

17. Who is Ashley's favorite solo artist?

18. What was Ashley's least favorite thing about filming *High School Musical*?

19. What was Ashley's first big purchase after landing her gig on *The Suite Life of Zack & Cody*?

20. What was Ashley's favorite activity when she was growing up?

Answers:

1. Her local mall; 2. July 2, 1985; 3. New Jersey; 4. A commercial for JCPenney; 5. Maddie Fitzpatrick; 6. Blondie; 7. Cancer; 8. Sharpay; 9. *Les Misérables*; 10. Creative writing; 11. Pink; 12. Sushi; 13. Jessica Simpson; 14. A Wet Seal salesgirl; 15. *Laguna Beach*; 16. Catherine Zeta-Jones; 17. Billy Joel; 18. Wearing high heels all the time!; 19. A condo; 20. Cheerleading

Chapter 17

Internet Resources

Ashley is a star who continues to shoot higher and higher. We know this girl isn't going to spend all her days lounging by the pool or shopping, no matter how much she adores those activities. We're talking about the actress who films movies in between TV shows! Her career is on the go, and she's loving every minute of it. By reading about how much happened to her in 2005 and 2006, you can see how quickly her world is changing. So if you want to stay on top of Ashley's latest news, head online and check out the following websites. They will definitely keep you current on everything happening in Ashley's life. You should always get a parent's permission before signing online, and keep in mind that websites are always coming and going!